PULSE

Writings on Sliabh Luachra

The Aisling or Dream in Real Life

Tommy Frank O'Connor

PULSE - Writings on Sliabh Luachra
is published by

DOGHOUSE
PO. Box 312
Tralee GPO
Co. Kerry
Ireland
Tel 066 7137547 email: doghouse312@eircom.net
www.doghousebooks.ie

October, 2006

168,189

ISBN 0-9552003-3-4 / 978-0-9552003-3-5

Edited for DOGHOUSE by Noel King

€12

(c) Tommy Frank O'Connor, 2006

Cover design: Stockbyte

Printed by Tralee Printing Works

Further copies available at €12, postage free, from the above address, cheques etc.
payable to DOGHOUSE also PAYPAL - www.paypal.com to
doghousepaypal@eircom.net

**Thanks for Kerry Group plc for their corporate sponsorship for this
volume.**

Doghouse is a non-profit taking company, aiming to publish the best of
literary works by Irish born writers. Donations are welcome and will be
acknowledged on this page.

for my mother Ellen

and
the Collins' of Counguilla, Scartaglin, Co Kerry

Acknowledgement is due to the editors / presenters / organisers of the following, where some of these works or versions of them were first awarded / broadcast / published: Acorn; The Bard Of Armagh; Bizz Buzz(India); The Brobdingnagian Times; Cavan Poetry Page; The Corvid Review(Canada); Cúirt Poets' Platform; First Edition; Haiku Headlines(USA); The Holly Bough; Legions Of Light(USA); Lumen; The Maine Event; Podium III; Quantum Leap; Radio Kerry; The SHOp; Start; The Stoney Thursday Book; The Jonathan Swift Awards; Talvipaivanseisaus (Finland); Wildeside; Words Unbound / Mots Déchainés.

The poems A Scent Of Music, Man Of Iron, The Master's Rest and Salmon Wake appeared in the author's poetry collection Attic Warpipes, (Bradshaw Books, 2005).

Thanks to Kerry County Library and to Eamon Browne of the Local History section.

Thanks to Cuman Luachra

Thanks to the Pádraig O'Caoimh Festival, Castleisland, Co. Kerry for the launch of this book.

Also by Tommy Frank O'Connor:

Novels;
The Poacher's Apprentice (Marino, 1997)

Kee Kee, Cup & Tok (Wynkn deWorde, 2004)

Poetry;
Attic Warpipes (Bradshaw Books, 2004)

Short Stories;
Loose Head (DOGHOUSE, 2004)

Contents

Introduction

This work attempts to reflect the philosophy of life of Sliabh Luachra.

So where is this place?

Geographically it stretches approximately from the Paps in the South to Lyrecompane in the North of County Kerry; it follows the Brown Flesk westwards to where it joins the river Maine and to the East it embraces that area of North Cork from Millstreet to Kanturk. Its influence however extends much further and seems to merge with areas of similar attitude such as Corca Dhuibhne (West Kerry), Uibh Ráthach (the Iveragh Peninsula, South Kerry), the environs of Carrigafoyle Castle, Ballylongford, that area of West Cork around Gougane Barra, Baile Mhuirne (Ballyvourney) and that part of Conemara west of Maam Cross.

What is peculiar about this way of life?

It's a matter of outlook. People here are in love with life but don't try to knock more out of it than is their due. Their predecessors knew the hunger of the stomach and learned that worrying about it was no help at all. They did find however that by coming together and addressing it in poetry, song, story and music they got the pain to work for them.

People here do not expect too much from life; they appreciate the difference between wealth and riches. All around them they see nature at work and have learned to observe its cycles. From a spring water well to a cobweb bejewelled with dew, they know that time just will not be rushed; it will however linger with those who are in tune with its pulse.

Swallows In The Rainbow

Victory and defeat are mere steps in the waltz of life. The ready acceptance of that idiom marks the main difference between those of a Sliabh Luachra frame of mind and those for whom winning is all that matters. In the latter mind-set, if you are not a winner you're a loser.

There are no losers in the Sliabh Luachra landscape. Here people who are down on their luck, battling with the bottle, grieving or trying to get their heads around a darkness or problem not of their own making are regarded as fellow travellers who, for the moment, need a little help with their cross. Nobody expects to find Paradise here, just a decent run at it so as to enjoy it all the better when the invitation comes to cross that horizon. Joy without sadness is like summer without winter.

This fellow-feeling, this responsiveness to the needs of others goes back at least to the time of Cromwell, but probably much further. To dear Oliver this heath of gorse, bog-cotton and rushes wasn't *Hell*; it wasn't even Connaught. He saw it as a place where snipe and curlew should be left to worm it out with the natives for the few miseries of life; it was not his scene. Some of those he dispossessed, particularly in the midlands, made their hungry journey to this place and found a way and view of life which defied hardship. Problems didn't seem quite so bad when shoulders, even more frail than one's own, willingly shared the burden.

By maintaining the tradition of burying each other's dead with dignity we continue to rekindle hope for the living. Dr. Albert E. Casey, an American Pathologist and son of a Knocknagree emigrant presented a treatise on the people of Sliabh Luachra to the International Academy of Pathology in San Francisco in 1969 on his scientifically established findings that these people had one of the longest and healthiest life spans in the world, in spite of a diet that should have had them joining the land of the dead some decades earlier than they do so.

People here know that whatever life might fling at them cannot be any worse than that borne by those who have gone before, those good people who enriched the part of the world they touched on their journey. I'm reminded of the man who was working on a Famine project in a local bog. The poor man was in fact closer to death from malnutrition than he realised. He was resting against the turf bank to keep himself standing when a well-fed ganger emerged out of the mist, accused him of idling and ordered him back to work.

'I'm not idling,' the man groaned, 'just waiting for a breeze to dry the turf.'

Mountain Man

I'm a son of Sliabh Luachra, no longer a boy,
I've worn leather a long way from Kerry.
I've been lonely in London and hungry at times
when my wages were used for being merry.
Those lucky in love soon find a good spouse,
as I did without knowing I was searching.
Her cooking, a home soon made of our house;
on my knees soon our children were perching.
The way to my heart she found through my gut,
from our home an aroma magnetic.
Not just food for appetised palates, but
something else that was rest from the hectic.
The happiness recipe everyone seeks,
I found in my family, each one unique.

The Sliabh Luachra free spirit is not uncaring; it has a genuine interest in the well-being of the other person; it is defiant in the face of misfortune or unfairness, it knows that the sun that waits to shine through the clouds will shed its beams without favour. Those who know how to interpret the rainbow also know how to find the treasure within.

Just two examples of this kind of spirit are my aunt Mary Collins of Counguilla, Scartaglin and her cousin the late Johnny 'The Tailor' Brosnan of that same village. As children they were victims of the polio epidemic of the late 1920's – early 30's. Life for many who survived this malady meant an existence wrapped in self-pity, unable to make a meaningful life for themselves. Not so for the afore-mentioned.

Mary had reconstructive work carried out in a Dublin hospital. coming and going over a number of years leaving her with one good leg. The other, though capable of bearing weight, never grew to catch up with the good one. So she decided to become a dressmaker, involving an apprenticeship in Castleisland, which she reached by bicycle. Those who know the road from Counguilla to Castleisland, and back, have an idea of the determination involved in that feat. On qualifying she set up business in Counguilla and later emigrated to Oakland, California where she worked as a seamstress, and has long since retired. Now in her eighty-eighth year she still makes her annual 12,000 mile round trip home to visit family and friends.

Moon-Struck

When last I travelled this way
I was going
where I am coming from,
facinated by what allures,
that will not leave me,

and inflames my rest.

Magic places twinkle,
bewitch my willing impulse
to seek their promise
and find their ways
criss-cross the same
as those I have already
found
wanting.

    The late Tailor Brosnan thought so little of his affliction that he
also trained to master the needle. He was then one of two tailors
in the village, the other one known as the 'old' Tailor, a great man
to whistle a tune and savour a *mejum* of stout and a nip of whis-
key. He was thus engaged in one of the local pubs one summer
evening when a group of American visitors stopped in. Fascinated
by the lilt and warble of his whistling, a lady came over from the
group and asked, "Sir, can I see your instrument?" The intent of
the question was slightly and deliberately misinterpreted by a few
of the local characters.

    But back to Johnny the 'young' Tailor, a most apt term indeed
for a man who never allowed the term 'old' to apply to him.
Having set up his business he decided to get others involved in his
love of music. He was also a great admirer of the patriot Thomas
Ashe, so he put the word around about forming a pipe band in
his name. Within days he had his men together. I don't know how

they acquired their instruments; it's likely that pleas for dollars were generously answered. A band needs somewhere to practice. While in the process of throwing a shed together beyond the junction on the Castleisland side of the village, Johnny decided they might as well build a dance hall as they were at it. And what name could he call that proud edifice only the Thomas Ashe Hall. Later the Daly brothers built the East End Ballroom, now a funeral home, opposite the church.

You can't run a dancehall without music. No bother to Johnny; sure he only had a tailoring business, a pipe band with its bookings and transport arrangements, and a dancehall to occupy his time. While his polio legs and auxiliary walking sticks wouldn't march with the Pipe Band, he certainly could lead a Dance Band as a drummer; that he did with considerable style and panache. There was no shortage of musicians keen to improve their style under the drumstick conducting of the master.

While Mary Collins remained single, Johnny courted and married Julie, his beautiful young wife from Castleisland. Together they found the time and not inconsiderable fun in enhancing the young population of the village. Unless I'm mistaken I believe he went on to play a part in bringing the 'Smith' O'Sullivans and the Flynn brothers together to form the Radiant Showband coming into the 1960's.

The film 'True Grit' would have no shortage of characters in this land. This is no place for a poser. The powdered peacock will find that his frippery is no more impressive than what flushes away when he pulls the chain in his lavatory. Even the clergy have had the occasional member a little over imbued with self importance. A Castleisland Canon now gone to his eternal reward, decreed that his parishioners would present themselves on time for Mass and that each would occupy a place in the pews; no more lounging down at the back or outside the door. He ensured compliance with his edict by parading outside the church when not saying Mass himself. One Sunday a lady from over two miles away arrived for the noon Mass five minutes after it had begun; after all what was the harm in stopping for a chat here and there along the way.

'And where do you think you're going?' the birettaed one bellowed.

'Did I ask you where you were going?' she countered, and walked on past him.

Pride is not always a deadly sin in Sliabh Luachra.

Most people of Sliabh Luachra know the stars and their place on the ground beneath. They know and cherish their music and musicians, their seanchaI (storytellers), singers and poets, their heroes in sport and family members who return from abroad to recharge their cultural batteries. Their world has many layers of wonder. Like W B Yeats in The Lake Isle of Innisfree, they ...*feel it in the deep heart's core*. This awareness balances pride with an innate sense of responsibility to the collective heritage.

Nowadays it is a joy to see so many young people carrying on and enhancing those traditions, encouraged by the many dedicated teachers and the parents and friends who give of their time to ensure that the best facilities are in place for this perennial flowering. Outlets such as the Scór na nÓg competitions organised and promoted by the Gaelic Athletic Association, the various Feiseanna (music and dance festivals) and local sessions bring them together to exchange tunes and compare styles. Like all who are good at what they do they make it look easy; you cannot help getting a sense of fun in the embrace of their welcome.

Not even here however will you find Utopia. The free-loader and vandal will not spurn opportunity anywhere, so people have had to adjust their trusting nature to this reality. The village that had two tailors and two dancehalls now has none. Times change;

while the villages have lost these aspects of life they have gained Cultural and Heritage Centres, better schools and sports facilities.

In this culture there is a generosity of spirit that not only survives but thrives in the ways people have time for each other, and in the love with which those who are gifted ensure that this talent is nurtured in the next generation.

scent of new-mown hay
awakens that summer youth
in the old woman

the spring-water well
hides within the overgrowth —
a cool memory

after the flowers
tuck their petals in to sleep
the night awakens

breeze in the ivy
whispers several secrets
to the listener

curlews curl
over the marshlands
— a lament

Land-Slip

As the world seems to become smaller, we learn within hours of major events everywhere. We can view natural disasters like hurricanes and volcanic eruptions almost as they happen. Other events like earthquakes and Tsunami arrive on our television screens and newspapers almost as quickly as it would have taken ink to dry a century ago. We thank our God for our good fortune as we cringe at our helplessness in the face of such devastation.

Imagine what it was like for the people of Knochnageeha and the surrounding countryside when they awoke on the morning of 28th December 1896. Very soon those who looked at the mire of sludge that had been house and homestead to the Donnelly family thanked their God that at least they were awake to see the horror. The Donnelly home and all who slept therein had been swept off the hillside overnight. It seemed that both parents and their seven children must have perished somewhere in that forbidding sludge.

Imagine what it must have been like for 13-year-old Katie Donnelly when she returned from an overnight visit to her grandmother to find no trace of the home and family she had left the day before. In those days of poor communications and no engineering equipment, the neighbourhood set about the task of finding the family under vast tonnage of quagmire and laying them to rest. They could pray that amid all of this at least one child had been saved. Later they learned that a dog and a duck also survived.

Katie went on to complete her formal education in the Loreto Convent Secondary School, Killarney. From there she went to London, then to Manchester where she met and married Killarney man Paddy O'Donoghue. One can only imagine the emotions of this resilient young woman as she and her husband were blessed with the start of their family in Manchester. Knocknageeha and its memories must have been reawakened with every toddle, smile and cry of their children.

They returned and built their home on the ground adjacent to where the Donnelly home had stood. There they added three more children to their two from Manchester and in due course Katie herself became a grandmother.

On 28th December 1996, Cumann Luachra along with those grandchildren and the wider community marked the centenary of that land-slip with a memorial to an event referred to locally as the Moving Bog Disaster.

More detail of this and other events can be read in the many issues of the excellent documentary and historical magazine *Journal Cumann Luachra*.

Genealogy Of Memory

I am the son of Poetry	Mac Filíochta is ea me;
Poetry, son of Reflection	Filíocht, mac Athmhachnamh;
Reflection, son of Meditation	Athmhachnamh, mac na Meabhraithe;
Meditation, son of Lore	Meabhr, mac Léann
Lore, son of Research	Léann, mac Taighde;
Research, son of Great Knowledge	Taighde, mac Eolas Iontach;
Great Knowledge, son of Intelligence	Eolas Iontach, mac Mheabhrach;
Intelligence, son of Comprehension	Meabhrach, mac Tuiscint;
Comprehension, son of Wisdom	Tuiscint, mac an Críonacht;
Wisdom, son of the Three Gods of Dana	Críonacht, mac na Trí Dia de Dana

A Master's Rest

in memory of Pádraig O'Caoimh, Master fiddler of Sliabh Luachra

Late at night when darkness gathers ramblers
round the embers, the roots of our musings
in tune with the dead, they request an air.

Pádraig takes the stretch of silence since
Aodhagán O'Rathaille, fathoms nadir of the heart
and heralds new pride in fiddle music.

His bow enchants old chords to resonate,
an aura in the flow breathes as a soul
flickers in memory; out of a throat

we hear a lyric *caoineadh* quiver
about 'O'Rathaille's Grave', imitate
a curlew winging music and maker

to some ancient craving in our marrow.
Silence a moment, like a tear falling
on a feather, the Master's eyes narrow

on the shape of sorrow. He weaves dignity
out of rags of regret for devil-may-care
lives, embalms their memory in gaeity.

A glass of porter banishes his blues,
for chase he plays a set of reels and polkas
into tired yawn of tomorrow's early hours.

Without a wife he has become groom
to his fiddle, a troubadour
drawing the cork out of the draught of gloom.

Parishes of pupils learn the power
of Heaven hiding in the gamut,
and sustain the heartbeat of Sliabh Luachra.

Caoineadh = Lament or Keen

Village Woman
for Bridie Galwey

In her sweetshop she observes the little faces,
snotty noses contemplating sixpence
worth of toffees, lucky bags or jelly babies
while clutching three-pence and a prayer that this
would multiply, like Jesus did with loaves and fishes.

Night-time neighbours gather in her kitchen,
the menu, a few games of thirty-one,
pots of tea with home-made scones or biscuits
but if any player's thoughts go for a ramble
they'll soon be homeward to a lashing tongue.

Music brings her back to all-night dances
with her blacksmith lover in a polka set,
they'd sing again the songs of their romancing
and thank whatever God made sure they met.

They'd marry and bring new life to the village;
a girl, a boy, another girl and then
the God who'd filled their happiness with riches
would call her husband to his requiem.

The pains of loss that nobody could measure
entwine like ivy round the grieving wife.
This darkest cloud, however, hid a treasure;
within her womb, the heartbeat of new life.

The village woman, born to be a mother,
stuck out her chin at life that seemed so cruel.
Her blacksmith's blacksmith wed her, and together
they added four more children to their pool.

Though fate again stole up and took her husband
and then returned to rob her eyesight too,
it could not spoil the village woman's vision,
nor could it cheat the love she had accrued.

One day a schoolboy asked her, in her sweetshop,
if postman brought her many Valentines?
Not a single card from anyone, she sighed.

The boy knelt on the floor and took a sweet box,
then tore a piece that fitted his design.
He thought about the feelings of the children,
then wrote the words he thought would do just fine:

If all the people who forgot to say "I love you"
sent a card, the postman would need help from Santa Claus

The Simpleton

As a trainee accountant in London from 1965 to 1968, I had to find work outside of the office to pay my way. I lived in Leytonstone, East London, so I applied to the Green Man, the biggest pub in the place, for part-time work. The *gov'nr* decided to interview me 'on the job', so he put me behind the counter of the public bar that Monday evening, showed me the price list and left me to work things out for myself. There were major road works under way in the area, so my clientele came from there and the local regulars.

My first problem was to figure out the local accents. What sounded like 'a lie in bed' was 'a light and bitter', i.e. a half pint of bitter ale topped off with a bottle of light ale; 'a brow–ma' was 'a brown and mild', again half-and-half of each. 'off a screw' or 'office crow' was 'half pint of scrumpy cider', and so on. The lads from the road works were mostly from Glasgow and Northern Ireland. Another interesting process to get the ear attuned to *those* accents. I learned quickly and got the job, introducing me to an academy of education that I still cherish.

Without realising it, I soon developed a way of associating client with pint, and an alertness for unspoken repeat orders, and became quite popular. The public bar backed on to the much bigger lounge which was out of bounds for me except on Saturday nights if it became too busy. I could still get a side light of some of the customers, particularly those seated at the bar. Among those, over at the corner to my left, I caught a glimpse one night of a man reading the Connaught Tribune. The lounge could have been empty for all the notice he took of anybody nearby. As far as I could see he managed to stretch a bottle of Guinness over the couple of hours of his stay.

A week later I was promoted to the lounge for Saturday night. At nine o'clock my man arrived, took off his overcoat and scarf and draped them over the stool on which he seated himself at the same place at the counter. His lean, tanned features suggested that he worked outdoors, though he lacked the rough gait of *the navvy*. He pulled a much folded Connaught Tribune from inside the belt of his trousers and placed it on the counter.

'A bottle of Guinness?' I suggested.

'Where's Martha?' He responded.

'On holidays, I think.'

'Oh,' he said and began to look over the paper, as if for the first time, but like he was double checking in case he'd missed anything. I took the liberty of opening a bottle and pouring it slowly in front of him, though he didn't seem to be looking. He put money on the counter. I took it and placed his sixpence change beside him. Three ladies arrived wrapped tightly in the bits they were wearing. Make-up, hair and nails must have taken ages. They slowly arranged themselves on stools at the bar while I served another group. The piano player told me that his drink for the night, whenever anyone was buying, would be Rum and Black; for now he was having a bottle of Guinness. I poured. The Tribune moved on to page two; the ladies flashed the lashes in a fit of the giggles and ordered two vodkas and orange and a Bloody Mary.

The *gov'nr* and his wife arrived. The ladies moved to a table opposite the door. I enquired of my man if he was from Connaught.

'Thereabouts,' he nodded. 'And you; what part are you from?' he enquired.

'Kerry, near Castleisland,' I said.

'Have nothing to do with them ones and their likes,' he indicated towards the giggles, just as the *gov'nr* drew me aside. He asked if I'd help out a *gov'nr* friend of his in a pub in Leyton for a few weeks; the man had to go up North to deal with some family matters. I asked for particulars. He told me to present myself at the Coach and Horses in Leyton when it opened the next day. The night became quite busy; the piano player scored ten Rums and Black, and my man decided I could call him Con. At a quarter to eleven he got off the stool, folded his newspaper before offering it to me, put on his scarf and coat and turned to leave.

'Your change,' I said, indicating the sixpence.

'I'll see you in Leyton,' he said, and pushed it towards me.

The few weeks in the Coach and Horses ran into months. Every Saturday night Con arrived and left to the same routine. While he chose not to disclose the exact part of Connaught he came from, he indicated that he'd not been back since his hurried departure some years earlier. Now about thirty years of age, he couldn't muster a single happy memory that might lure him back.

'Your parents; your family?' I suggested.

'Never knew who they were,' he said, without trace of regret.

'But you must have feelings for someone back there; maybe a girl like Martha from the Green Man?' He pretended not to hear this.

In that pub and at the dances, I saw how the frame of mind of the emigrant influenced subsequent feelings for home. Those who left embittered, feeling that the country had let them down, tended to forget or try not to remember anything about home. On Friday nights the sight of men, old before their time, mumbling as they contemplated their pints, prompted me to try to engage with them.

Con never wept in his glass of stout. I asked why he'd followed me to the Coach and Horses. 'Because you keep asking me questions without saying a word; questions I should be asking of myself,' he almost smiled. It was then he told me of his work as a forester'

'For as long as I can remember I could grow anything I wanted;

"you could grow an oak in a thimble of ashes," the only kind teacher I ever had, said to me before I was fostered'.

On Friday at the pub and Sunday nights at the dances, I listened to stories of mid-week and winter hunger, of night plodding after hopeless day, of slavish dedication to a work routine with little or no enduring financial reward, of fathers who resented the freedom of their children to leave, of mothers and grandparents who wished them well and hoped in due course they'd share their good fortune with those left behind. And while their mothers were alive they'd put a bit by to get home for Christmas each year. At home they'd lie about the good life in England. The only truth might be of the great money they earned. They hid the reality of their longing for meaning in their lives, of just wishing to be somebody, of finding a woman with the patience of their mothers who could help them to put words on their pain and then treat it with generous dollops of love and affection.

These men failed to see or heed the irony in the pointless routine into which they'd fallen, the very thing from which they'd fled. Fortunately, it was only the few emigrants who drifted into this misery-go-round existence. Those who looked up from their shovels tended to see the clusters of opportunities awaiting exploration. In the England of the 1960's what you could do, or dared to try, was more important than who you were. Courage tended to yield new promise from each sunrise for those who followed the dream.

Con had heard of Epping Forest as a boy, so when he got off the train in Euston, he enquired how to get to Epping. Soon he was on a Central Line Underground train which took him all the way there. He was offered a job with the use of a cabin while he settled in. I'll never forget the satisfaction in his eyes as he told how it felt to be putting away real money in the bank every week.

'So you have a dream?' I asked.

'Don't you?' He countered.

Many emigrants from Sliabh Luachra brought their own salvation with them. Those who couldn't play music could dance, sing or tell stories, so they found themselves in a much warmer social circle. In the course of their sessions in Kilburn, Camden Town, or across the Atlantic in The Bronx, San Francisco or wherever they found themselves in the world, they'd enquire about their strays, find them and coax them back into the fold. For these emigrants, home was ever present in their consciousness; they'd find it not only in their music, song and story but also in the newspapers from home. It was to people like these that a young Fr. Eamon Casey turned for help in the early days of getting a refuge going for those who had fallen on hard times and a reference point for new arrivals.

A new arrival or a visitor was guaranteed a special welcome, so as to share the news about the people in the parish, village or town-land. Who had the stations? Who was there? Who had died, married or had increases in the family? Who else had emigrated and to where? Did anyone come home and settle, buy a farm, maybe reconnect with an old romance? Was it true that more people were going to college? Was so-and-so still doing the post? Who from the area was on the Kerry or Cork football teams? Was there any improvement in business or in the jobs situation?

Meanwhile Saturday nights came and went. My sixpenny tip from Con extended to whatever I was having myself. He seemed to learn more about me than I of him, though I could feel the pain as he waded through the story of how at school he was treated as if the circumstances of his speculative conception and birth were his own doing. Outside of school, some of the names he was called were hard to believe. He soon realised that it was easier to adopt the role of simpleton in which he was cast than to betray any signs of the many lessons he was learning.

'But you must have had some sort of a home life, Con?'

'Fostered to an elderly couple that lost the only son they had to the water. Blamed me for it after a while, though he drowned before I was born.'

'You can't be serious?'

'He's not our Michael, they'd complain, and hit me if I was within reach. The woman would weep and beat me with her rosary beads at night.'

'How or why did you leave?'

'The old man was crippled with pains; couldn't do much so I had to work all hours to get jobs done. One night after securing the cows in new aftergrass, I heard a commotion under the bridge. I peeped under and saw a girl I knew being interfered with by two blokes. I knew them lads too; posh but bad articles. She didn't want or welcome what they were trying to do, so I rushed in, grabbed the blokes and told the girl to run off home. I managed to get their heads under the water, otherwise I couldn't have held on to them. But they threatened me that if the girl reported it, they'd say they chased *me* off her, that plenty had seen me talking to her after Mass on Sundays and so on. Anyway who'd believe any story I told and who wouldn't believe them; "two against one", they crowed.'

'So you left?'

'I took their motorbike and whatever cash they had on them and was on the first boat to Hollyhead next morning.'

'And what did you do with the bike?'

'Rolled it off the pier; enjoyed that splash, so I did.'

'You didn't think of selling it?'

'And give away where I might be gone? Anyway I had more money off them blokes than I'd have in a year from the old people.'

'So that's why you get the Tribune, checking on news of those people?'

'One of those blokes came to a bad end. The other took over his father's business; very big shot now, according to himself.'

'And the girl?'

'She went to work for the old couple. Saw them to their grave.' I noticed something close to a 'what if?' glistening in his eyes. I observed him as I set up a few trays of orders for customers, the way he tapped his fingers on the Connaught Tribune he'd left on the counter for me to take away later. Con's demeanour indicated that a woman had nudged something in his mind.

'Your name is not Con, is it?'

'How'd you figure that out?'

'It's Michael, isn't it? That's why the old couple complained that you were not *their* Michael; yet they wanted a boy named Michael. And maybe when they saw how loyal you were to them they missed their might-have-been son all the more.'

'I think I'll have another bottle of stout,' he sighed.

As I poured it and set it to settle, he asked what I would do about going back to the only place he knew as home, bad and all as it was, now that the old people had left it to the girl. I looked at him, looked deep into those eyes that had tried to hide so much pain. I didn't have to ask the question that prompted itself; there was a memory, one fond hope from which he could not run away.

A smile played on his lips.

Resurgence

On a visit back from the world they meet
as each trails a gather of memories.
Along by the brook they find new love still
young after flyaway years: loyal streams

busy trickling over stones and pebbles
whisper secrets of the night; in sunshine
dancing in the light; in moonbeams, silver
with stars. In his eyes she's now a woman

ripened in the promise of her fledging,
while she beholds the boyfriend who has filled
her dreams. They cuddle back the years before
they cross the bridge and take that table

in the café nook. He wonders how she can
remember little things like one sugar
and the milk she pours into his cup
before the tea. They drink each other's eyes.

He notices that she still takes hers black
and sips a younger sweetness – not having
tasted sugar in over twenty years.
Outside again they find themselves beneath

the sycamore blooming in the rising
sap springing through tree-trunk rings of decades
seasoning the mystery of rebirth.
She hearkens as he whispers pictures

from their secret summer when scents of dawn
awoke in blissful dew, then pollinated
country days with meadow-sweet, woodbine, wild
ditches of blossoms gilding leaf and thorn.

Their taste buds again to ambrosial
strawberries they fed one by one to each
other, verged with the ruddy zing of sloes.
Their evening vigil lingers while petals

enfold their dreams reborn in sunset.

Ranaleen Rambles

Decimal currency was twenty-seven years distant when I was born in Ranaleen in 1944. World War II still had eighteen months destruction to accomplish, culminating in the atomic bombing of Hiroshima and Nagasaki. Éire, in its 1937 Constitution, was seven years old, and rural electrification was almost nine years into the future.

It was a pastoral time. Men and women, hardened to the toil of making a living, retained a soft core of sentimentality. People mattered; they had an identity. They closed ranks in times of crisis; for bereavements, to cope with a run of bad luck. They came together in rejoicing at stations; weddings; the return of an emigrant. Life ambled along in a pony & trap, on bicycles, around Bernie's wet-battery radio as Micheál Ó'Hehir described the stirring deeds of our heroes. People went to their graves never having journeyed beyond Killarney for the races, Killorglin for Puck Fair, or perhaps the rare journey on the steam ghost train from Farranfore to an All-Ireland final.

One who left Ranaleen thirty years ago pens these memories. In my travels through England, Scotland, Wales, Europe and the USA, I have been proud to remember that I started in Ranaleen, that townland at the eastern end of the parish between Clounreeney and Inchincummer, with the Brown Flesk to the north and Banaglanna and Gloundaeigh climbing over the hill to the south where we cut our turf in the sweeping view of Killarney lakes and mountains.

Looked at objectively, there was poverty in our lives. But there was a richness and resourcefulness in our way of life that defied our economic conditions. A tradition of co-operation (cúmhairing), common to most rural communities, reduced problems to manageable proportions. God helped those who showed an inclination to help themselves. One of my earliest memories is of Ration Books, tea being the principal commodity. Coffee was unheard of in our area before 1952. Scarcity tends to focus the mind. In common with many of our rural colleagues we looked to our resources and discovered opportunity. We raised our own food. Each household had at least one wooden tub bound with hoops, which could be used for pickling, or for mixing the bluestone and washing soda to spray the potato garden. One or two pigs would be killed each year.

Irish Recipe

The hill smiles back at the sun, just as her stories said
when Boston neighbours called
to taste the Irish woman's food,
and borrow recipes for bread.

Her table, an altar for body and soul, fed
lilting images of mountains
in a kingdom far away, but native
to the warm voice and smiling eyes of my mother.

At home we joined her prayers
that empty hearts be filled with God's peace;
that pain, undetectable to scan or X-ray,
be coaxed from lonely hiding places.

Plans to feast her eyes, her taste,
on homeland ways, postponed year after year
to feed the hungers of those who never knew
barefooted freedom in river, bog or meadow.

Now I understand why this place danced
in every beat of her heart. Each day a seasonal sun
kisses the convex face of that towering hill,
caressing her ashes to its heathered breast.

I trace recipes, alive in their sources,
treasures to daughters from mothers' hands.
Wheat, sage, bay-leaf, thyme,
sustaining Irish homes in foreign lands.

Tommy, my father, wielded the butcher's knife in Ranaleen. The table would be brought from the kitchen into the yard. A few neighbours and the hired workman would hold the pig, while the women would be ready to capture the blood in enamel buckets. Tommy would make the sign of the cross on the pig's throat with the tip of the knife, then a quick cut and thrust straight to the heart. Activity for the next hour was frantic. A full and half tub were on standby; the full tub contained about ten gallons of boiling water. Intestines were removed for cleaning in the yard; the women took organs and pork steak straight to the kitchen. The pig was dipped in the boiling water, and removed for shaving by the men using butchers knives and old cut-throat razors. Again the pig was dipped and cleaned before Tommy cut it into joints and sections for salting and pickling in the tub, later to hang on hooks from the rafters in the kitchen.

Meanwhile chopped onion, blended cereal, herbs and spices were mixed with the blood and filled into the cleaned intestines by the women. Simmering pork steak, kidneys, heart and liver sent an aroma into the yard to excite even the most delicate palate. The cats and dogs of the neighbourhood congregated in expectation. But the men were not quite ready. Rising thirst had to sample a mug of porter from the quarter tierce before approaching the kitchen table laden with boiled spuds, raw onions cut in rings, and plates from the simmering pot dressed with swedes and/or cabbage. Milk was taken as required in mugs out of the gallon.

Black puddings now simmered in two pots hanging from the crane over the extended fire. When ready, they were taken out with the tongs and hung on brush-handles to set. Some were later wrapped in parcels for each house in the neighbourhood. A bit of pork steak might be included for relatives or special friends further afield.

The quarter tierce came into its own for all meitheal activities such as killing the pig, threshing, and maybe digging the potatoes. Stations and wakes might require two, and no American wake got into swing until the mallet drove the tap into the barrel. I was always fascinated by the facility of the black stuff to get the conversation going among the men, just as the drop from the red bottle sent words and giggles spinning among the women.

Hens provided the main source of argument between my mother and father. He maintained that no hen ever paid her way. She made sure we collected the eggs, which were exchanged for goods in the local shop. A hen hatching at the wrong time would be steamed and placed under a bucket to serve a cooling-off period. This was guaranteed to bring her back to productivity in the flock. Hens that had served their purpose would be despatched to Lane's truck on its monthly visit to Dunleavy's shop, there to join other hens for whatever awaited them in Cork. My mother liked to experiment with fowl. Ducks, geese, turkeys, even the more exotic guinea hens, all had their time and place in our farmyard, to my father's increasing consternation.

A classic conflict between the perspectives of price and value. The fate of the egg-sucking cat bears witness to the relative values: suspect was observed on a number of occasions scurrying from the hen house leaving evidence of cracked and almost empty egg shells. The number of eggs available to the household reduced as his taste and body sheen increased. Several efforts to catch him failed. A loan of Charlie's shotgun, a single cartridge, aim and fire. He fell from the tree, all nine lives gone in one bang. Joan wondered if we could be absolutely sure he was the culprit. Helen stamped her foot on his stomach. The offending evidence gushed out.

Rabbits contributed to the local economy right through the fifties. Paddy Broderick of the Lake was the agent, and all rabbits presented had to be panced (cleaned out). He would reserve the right to refuse any that weren't up to standard. It was not unusual for an ancient skinny buck to have his shoulders and quarters padded out with wet newspaper. Those rabbits prepared many houses for stations, lined a sack for Santa Claus, and fitted out emigrants for a start in England or the USA. But the rabbits became a pest, an enemy of progress in agriculture. Myxomatosis was introduced, and eradicated them for almost twenty years.

Secret Ingredient

Welcome into my mountain Kingdom here,
you'd like again that mystery to explore
of how, within my bounds and rugged shore,
so many find rebirth each passing year.
It's in the air a goodly group insists,
while some advance the way we hold our drink.
The water from my mountains crowned in mist
is what gives Kerry life its health, some think.
My people thrived on salty sides of pig,
hung on hooks from seasoned smoky rafters.
Today their diet sees them skip a jig,
laughter still their favoured dish for afters.
Wholesome food, a drop of cheer so merry,
simple things enrich our lives in Kerry.

Electricity, the stations, and whooping cough arrived at the same time, around 1952 or thereabouts. I remember Jim Collins from Ardfert wiring the house (later to be extended by Con Dennehy). Jackie Griffin of Dromulton carried out renovations.

My mother worked mottle-effect painting into panels over the hearth and up the stairway. A bout of whooping from the baby would see mother dropping everything, snatching her from the pram out into the air and helping her struggle through. We would pray that the blue taint on the baby's skin on such occasions would fade to normal; thank God it always did. My abiding memory of those stations is the number of times I had to bring a specially adapted butter box from the small room upstairs, empty the vessel out in the dungheap, and steal the contraption back upstairs as unobtrusively as possible. All the while Fr. Counihan collected and recorded the Station dues.

A regular visitor who always seemed to arrive a day after excitement settled was Paddy O'Brien, one of the last great tinker men. It would take him a few days to work his way through the townland, repairing and making tin gallons and utensils in welcoming households. In latter years he would use two sticks to assist his arthritic progress, but never lost his sense of humour. I'll never forget his response on one occasion after my father eased him into the high armchair near the hearth.

'And how are you keeping these times, Paddy?'

'Yerra how would I be keeping, going to bed barefooted and getting up fasting?'

The 1953 All-Ireland football final between Kerry and Armagh stirred Ranaleen in a special way. John Joe Sheehan of Farranfore, a first cousin of the Flynns, was playing on the forty. We all gathered around Bernie O'Connor's wet-battery radio as Mícheál O'Hehir described Armagh's Mal McEvoy soaring head and shoulders over them all. Apart from John Joe Sheehan, other heroes such as Mixie Palmer, John Cronin and captain Jas Murphy entered folklore on that day, winning 13 points to 1-6, the first of Kerry's three All-Irelands of the 1950's. Peter McDermott's Meath were too good for us the following year 1-13 to 1-7, but we won't forget Mícheál O'Hehir's description of the Meath captain as 'the man with the cap'. One of the sweetest victories of all followed in 1955 when a young John Dowling captained our underdogs against

a Dublin team relying heavily on the terrible-twin axis of Ollie
Freaney and Kevin Heffernan. But John Cronin and Eddie Roche
unhinged the axis, and forwards like Paudie Sheehy, Jim Brosnan
and Tadghie Lyne bore Sam Maguire home – 12 points to 1-6.

Ear's Eye

The world outside inside a box,
hailstone-crackle to Athlone eekle-weekle,
we are one with wireless voices.

I clean my nose, enquire – *why so many wires for a wireless?*
There's news about the rationing, I'm wise as ever.

A tune, a sign, a scrape of chairs clears a space
for minds to cobble images from words
with home-made faces.

Night-ride Europe, a Luxembourg detective masons up a case
in tones that tell us he's the boss, but will he win this?

A summer Sunday, Croke Park heads in a rosary
of villages hushing for their parish player
to score the winner.

On holidays, car radio scouts among the channels
for a home view of the world.
Our mind's eye listens.

Our local school was Kilsarcon. We pestered our parents each
Spring to be allowed to go barefoot. A week or two before permission was granted, a group of us would hide our footwear (welling-
tons or boots) on the way to school and step into them again on
our shortcut home through the fields. We all got a great start from
Miss Daly, continued on through second and third classes with
Mrs. Foran, and then on to the larger-than-life Seamus Murphy for
fourth onwards. Having gone through it themselves, it was a treat
for fifth and sixth to observe Seamus introducing the new fourths

to the proper delivery of poetry and song during first term each year. Beecher's Brook was in the first line of 'The Old Priest Peter Gilligan': *the Old Priest Peter Gilligan was weary night and day...* The words had to be distinctly enunciated, particularly pronouncing the *d* in and followed by the *d* in day. The trick in singing was to open the mouth so that two fingers standing on edge could fit in. How many tears of frustration and laughter flowed over that one! But Seamus had a way with the odd funny story to lighten the effort, such as his recipe for the three fastest ways to send a message: Telephone, Telegraph and Tell a Woman!

After fourth class I moved to Ranalough where I completed fifth, sixth and seventh under Tim Keane. While I was in fifth class the parish was stunned with the sudden death of my uncle Paddy, the very popular blacksmith. I remember Freddie Galwey coming into the school porch and an ashen-faced Master asking me to go straight home. The strongest man in the community had no answer to a blood clot to the brain, leaving Bridie widowed with three young children, and expecting her fourth – Patrick, now a welder in New York. Freddie carried on the business in the forge and later married Bridie. They had their own family of whom Michael is a world famous Rugby International and, like his uncle Mick, is a former county gaelic footballer.

Man Of Iron

I was ten the day the world stopped.

A pallid neighbour beckoned the Master
to our classroom door. They whispered, shook heads.
Ashen Master took my hand; trembling,
he gave me to the messenger
who sent me pedalling home.

It's uncle Paddy, my mother said;
he's dead, a blood clot to his head.

Not my uncle Paddy, I cried;
remembering what the priest had said
on Sunday when thanking him for the gates
and railings he had made for the church.

Red-hot iron obeyed his hammer,
went to work as horseshoes,
wheel-bands, gates, railings.
Broken things lived again
after his hands mended them.

His death gathered in the village
around the house. A man, they said,
who did not know his power.
Voices found themselves without words
horses and carts stole by

on hooves and wheels he'd shod.
The black forge silent. So young, they sighed.
I cried with neighbours I'd thought dry
of tears, lingered, touched his hands
scrubbed white of smoke: cold, hard as iron.

Why? The raw question wailed,
the high sun burned
still no answer,
only my boy-offering –
> *there's no blacksmith*
> *among the Apostles*
> *and they need the best*
> *to make new railings for Heaven.*

For some time before that, falling mortar and rising damp in the old chapel concentrated the mind of the parish on the financing and building of a new church on a site provided by the Meredith estate at the back of the old chapel. Fathers Counihan and McSweeney brainstormed every possible means of raising money. Emigrants were informed of our plight in a way that hinted they should respond in kind. A levy system was devised on a cow head-age basis, and another system for those in other employment or business. Those who tried to cheat the system soon gave up when subscribers' names and amounts were read out at all Masses. Any loose money that was left was got at through 'draws' and 'silver circles'. I remember an occasion when our family had a good run picking blackberries, sold at Joan Fitz's for 4/=(30c) per stone. We had accumulated over £3 when collectors arrived for the monthly instalment, leaving us with only a half-crown (16c).

When the local branch of the National Farmers Association was formed my father was elected honorary secretary, and began to nib-ble on ideas of progressive farming. This would sometimes involve reading and writing into the night. The volume increased when the idea of forming a Co-operative Livestock Mart in Castleisland was floated. It was fundraising time again, this time in the form of Share Capital. The days of the fair were numbered, although it took the sceptics a while to recognise that. A fat heifer around that time, 1956/57 would do well to make £55; a fat cow £45; a fat sheep £8, while you could get a good fat lamb for £7. The ideal weight of a factory pig was 12 stone 12 lbs, while a pig for the table should weigh nearer 15 stone. The factory pig would make £18 and the one for the table £20 to £22. The bonham to start all over again would cost £5-10/ to £7.

In Ranaleen we bought our bonhams in litters of ten to twelve, and at one time would have had sixty pigs at different stages of fattening. Bacon connoisseurs regard those days as the time of real bacon when the staple diet of a growing pig was skim milk, Rhyno No. 1 & 2, supplemented with various greens, potatoes and root crops as supply would allow. The pig for the table would be finished on fodder beet, cabbage, nettles, peel of swedes, potatoes, apples and steamed barley. The fat of that bacon had a solid texture and needed no additives to dress the cabbage or swedes for taste between tongue and palate.

Household and livestock benefited simultaneously from the advent of running water. The diviner's rod dipped sharply over a convenient spot at the back of our henhouse; a rig moved in and punched a 120-ft. hole, lining it with pipes as it went. A water pump was wired up, and plastic pipes extended inside the back door of the kitchen and to the water trough in the yard. No more hauling from the well. Our twins Helen and Mary had the job at that time, drawing two buckets a day. Helen would argue that as she brought the buckets to the well, Mary should bring them back up! Mary soon learned.

Dairy herds at that time were mostly shorthorn, with the occasional Kerry or Whitehead cross. It was customary to have a goat running with the herd for fertility and good luck, though many a goat was cursed for chewing shrubbery and lingerie that were definitely out of bounds. Many remedial qualities were attributed to the goat's milk, particularly for chest complaints and recovery from serious illness. But the casualties of progress are many. The campaign to eradicate tuberculosis discouraged having goats mixing with the herd. Very few cows in Ranaleen reacted, but the goats had to go. The term 'reactor' entered local folklore, and was attributed to failure in any endeavour. At the time a local bachelor with many shroves on the clock was trying without success to find a suitable life partner. His endeavours, however, were confined to the local polka competitions in the Macra na Feirme Hall. On a night when his set did not impress the judges, and the woman of his dreams did not land in his arms, a local wag remarked 'reactor again tonight, Mikey?' (not his real name).

In the late fifties, a push to increase milk production was initiated by the Dairy Disposal Board. We bought an in-calf Friesian heifer from Charlie Lenihan's famous herd. She was the first in Ranaleen and cost twice as much as a shorthorn. True to her breeding she produced twice the gallonage of milk over a longer lactation period. Neighbours came to observe her at close quarters, some remarking that her udders were even bigger than those of an over-endowed elderly maiden in a neighbouring townland. This heralded a revolution; the bull with the ring on his nose came head to head with *the bull with the collar and tie*. The new bull didn't eat grass, and raced through the countryside in a cream-coloured Volkswagen from his base in Castleisland. Artificial Insemination (A.I.) brought the semen of well-bred Friesian bulls: cross-fertilised with the native shorthorn, the reds and greys gave way to the black and whites. One vicious banín defiantly held her place in the production stakes despite the stress of a rope and tubular spancel to prevent her from kicking bucket and milker into the next byre. Our cows were milked by hand while we were in Ranaleen. If we had the first Friesian, Charlie McSweeney next door had the first milking machine, the first tractor – a grey Ferguson, and his sister Sheila had the first motor car – a Ford Prefect, to which the cob would sometimes be tackled to get it started. Motorised transportation quickly took over, and soon our pigs were being taken to market in Mickey Fleming's pick-up truck. But farming methods retained their labour intensity, maintaining the era of the servant boy and girl for a few more years. Later, of course, the EEC brought many changes.

Milk Edict

More milk, more milk we squeezed into our buckets.
More milk, more milk from tough or tender paps.
More milk, more milk the cry from the Department,
Milk more, milk more, there's money in those teats.

Cull your Shorthorns; cull your Whiteheads, Kerries, Angus too.
Cull your bulls not specially bred for milk or beef, adieu.
Cull your buildings not designed for modern milking cows.
Cull the folks who shy away from fat long-term loans.

More lactation, specialisation, they even eyed my wife.
More awareness of production, cows now black and white.
More variety of breeding, the bull is called A. I.
More directives, regulations dominate our lives.

Drop those silly names of cows, numbers are the business.
Drop your money in the Bank to meet the standing orders.
Drop your paperwork on time to various State Departments.
Drop your pants, the Tax Collector must inspect your assets.

Cut back; cut back the Intervention Mountain.
Cut back, change tack the bureaucrats demanding.
Cut back, quota smacked to regulate the system.
Cut back, health freaks link up high cholesterol.

Butter Mountain, Meat Mountains, Wine Lakes rising,
Third World refugees, famine victims starving.
Bureaucrats, fat cats decree it is the system
They're there, we're here, politics the problem.

Set-aside hitherto working fertile acres.
Fallow minds, blinkered eyes see one side of problem.
Flip side, people dying is someone else's business.
People really are a bother, exercising freedom.

Farm folks, old hands stuck in their tradition.
Growing crops, weather forecasts dominate their vision.
Goat's milk, free-range eggs now are all illegal.
Bureaucrats laughing stocks, goats or hens don't heed you.

Bureaucrats have the knack of justifying existence.
Regulations need enforcement, so we've more officials.
More of officials need officials for administration.
Milk more; milk more taxes from the payer.

A very prominent man on our landscape in the fifties and sixties
was Denny (Dan Hugh) McSweeney and his blue Fordson Major
tractor. Johnny O'Connor of Dromulton had a red David Browne
with a reaper and binder and mowing bar, but Denny had the full
works, including plough, rotovator and threshing machine. Rats
and ghost stories added an extra dimension to the threshing
which by nature was an autumnal activity. Rats liked to nest under
the ricks of corn, feeding on the kernels falling off the sheaves. The
dogs – terriers in particular – sensed their presence. As the ricks
were opened up and lowered, as the sheaves were tossed on to the
threshing machine, the rats would make a run for it. A quick grind-
ing snatch in a dog's jaws ended the dash. The dogs hated those
rats, not even touching them with their lips as they tossed them
from their mouths. The day of the threshing meant a day home
from school for the older children, to help around the house with
all that feeding a meitheal involved. When it ran into the night the
meitheal would sip their porter in the yard, then gather around the
fire as the oil lamp would be lit. After recounting stories and yarns
from other threshings, the conversation would drift to great men of
old, patriots, weight-throwers, tug-of-war men, footballers, runners.
Names like Stack, Danno Mahony, Buddy Sugrue, the Casey broth-

ers, Austin Stack, Humphrey Murphy, John Joe Sheehy, and Dick Fitzgerald interspersed with songs like 'The Valley of Knockanure', 'Kevin Barry', 'The Three Flowers', and 'Richard Shanahan, John Prendeville and Flynn'. I can well remember crouching at the top of the stairs listening to the ghost stories when I was supposed to be in bed. The atmosphere and effects were just right: the glow from the fire, the flame from the lamp dancing in each draught, shadows keeping time around the walls; the smoke from the pipes drifting past me out the landing window; the smell of the stout as the talk got louder. But then it would hush for stories of change-lings; of hunts galloping over fields and ditches, leaving no tracks; of banshees wailing their announcement of impending death in certain families; of the recent dead coming back at Halloween; of music coming from the old fort in our cathair field coinciding with old seasonal festivals such as mid-summer, St. John's eve, 23rd June. Piseógs and their remedies were discussed, particularly in the context of the St. John's eve fire. There were indeed strange and not entirely unfounded beliefs then. The one about not walk-ing under a ladder challenged something inside me when John Horan's ladder leaned against Kilsarcon school while he replaced a few slates. I repeatedly walked under that ladder while a few girls proclaimed as gospel that "Francie'll grow no more". They were only partly right: my stunted growth stopped just short of 6' 2"!

But electric light and Radio Luxembourg chased the ghosts away. 208 meters medium wave found a wide audience through Perry Mason, and held on to the youth with Bing Crosby, Perry Como, Connie Francis, Lonnie Donegan, Elvis, Cliff, Ricky Nelson, Grace Kelly, and many more. At that time Radio Eireann closed down early, leaving a gap readily filled by 208.

About May 1957, Fr. Sean McSweeney encouraged the schools

of the parish to get involved in football leagues. He wanted to run trials for a parish team to participate in the Castleisland under-16 District League. Liam Dennehy and I had already developed a good understanding as goalkeeper and full-back respectively on the Ranalough school team, and in the summer of 1958 we filled these positions for Currow. Older members of the team included Mick Fleming, Pat and John Scanlon, but most – such as Con Riordan and Bertie Scanlon, were turning fourteen like ourselves. We played Desmonds, Ballymac, Cordal, Knocknagoshel and Brosna, winning all our games and conceding only two goals, if I remember rightly. Our means of transport were bicycles, Fr. Sean's and Billy Walsh's cars and Mick Culloty's van.

The open sports were a major annual event, attracting athletes and cyclists from all over Munster. The road cycle race always started the event: Currow–Scartaglin–Castleisland back up to the village. Dan Aherne dominated those races, hard pressed by Johnny Drumm, and Johnny Brosnan. I cannot remember the iron man – Mick Murphy of Caherciveen, but others who were prominent included the Laceys and Griffins of Tralee, with Brendan Brosnan and Lawrence Curtin of Castleisland. On the track they would later tangle with specialists and national champions such as Fermoy's Frank O'Sullivan, Cappoquin's Tom O'Neill, and the Crowleys of Blarney. Athletes from Castleisland's golden era such as Dave Geaney, Brendan O'Rourke, Mick Murphy, Ronnie and Mick Brosnan held their own against Tralee's Jerry Kelliher, Sean Hennessy, Seamus O'Mahony and Christy Murray, Tom O'Riordan of Ardfert, Tim and Tony Griffin of Ballymac, Tony Nolan of Limerick, the Naughtons of Nenagh, Willie Webb and Willie Neenan of Cork, Moss O'Connell of Moyvane and Croom's Mick Manning. In the field events our own Denny McSweeney, Martin Culloty and

Tom Donnellan did battle against Listowel's Eddie Leahy, Tadgh Justice of Millstreet, Croom's renowned Paddy Ruddle, the Beasley brothers from Rising Sun, among others. My proud and abiding memory of those tussles is of Denny powering his way over them all to victories in shot, 56 lbs. for distance and over the bar, with Martin and Tom mixing it right to the end.

Our local Rambling House was Rosie Flynn's, a fine musician on fiddle or concertina with exactly the right blend of roguery and grace. In a house like that, you learned to dance without really trying. Beneath the banter and the *leg-pulling*, the newcomer was nurtured into mastery of polka, waltz and quickstep, assuming that both legs were reasonable comrades and co-ordinated from a brain that could count in variations of 1-2-3. It was from Rosie's that the Biddy (the St. Brigid's day version of the Wrenboys) would start. There too the Biddy dance would be held in the middle of February each year, Connie Fleming helping Rosie with the music. That local group was well established before I was old enough to join. In fact the younger group started some time after Seanie Flynn received the contents of a 'po' from the upstairs window of a house that did not want to receive the Biddy.

The 'po' or chamber pot was the poor man's alternative to boiling oil. We carried it on after that for a while, giving that house a wide berth. I can remember the ease with which otherwise shy lads would sing their songs behind a Biddy mask: Seanie Flynn's 'Noreen Bawn' stands out. Our younger group sang songs such as 'The Stone Outside Dan Murphy's Door' – usually adapted to the house we were in, such as 'The Stone Outside Jeff Nagle's Door', 'Courting in the Kitchen', and 'The Garden Where The Praties Grow'. Flor O'Mahony and Florry Flynn ably demonstrated that lady who *walked throughout the world without the Grecian bend.*

Lent, Ling and Acting are comrades of memory. The Black Fast of Ash Wednesday, each Friday, and throughout Holy Week: one main meal of potatoes, vegetables and ling – a dried salted fish so tough it would have made soles for boots if you could drive tacks through it. Dances or weddings were not allowed during Lent, so variety shows and plays found their season. The local drama group would put on a play such as 'The Troubled Bachelors'.

Touring companies came into their own at this time, setting up tent in Tom Shanahan's field. Comedy, melodrama and tragedy always included the tear-jerker 'East Lynn'; not a dry eye in the house on the second last night. Everybody was back for the comedy on the final night; not a dry seat in the house. Sometimes the medicine man would ply his cure-all bottle; usually liquorice flavoured poteen masquerading as a healing elixir. But if you were off the drink for Lent, who could begrudge you a drop of medicine!

Our near neighbours, Charlie and Bernie, both had orchards. I never had any difficulty understanding the problem of the forbidden fruit for Adam and Eve. The ultimate temptation to me, at ten or eleven, was those juicy balls of flavour presenting themselves to the sun on the topmost branches. A quick raid on Charlie's orchard produced a few which brought me back for more. I think it was his sister Lizzie's voice addressed me from beneath the tree on which I had reached the top on the next occasion.

'Just the lad I was looking for; I can't get anyone to climb a tree around here, and I need this filled.' She produced a flourbag! That took all the good out of Charlie's, so my next raid was on Bernie's. The tree I had in mind was very high, but oh, what temptation. Help I had tried to recruit failed to materialise. Those apples away up there were too luscious to leave, so on my own I climbed and shook, not realising that I had a hidden audience of Bernie and some of the lads who would not join in my efforts. I climbed down, made a makeshift bag out of my shirt, and loaded up. I was tasting the first one when Bernie sauntered up to me. I proffered one; he accepted. I offered opinions on the weather and sundry affairs of the day as we left the orchard, and then I took my plunder home. Never since have I tasted apples like those, but my parents sent me back with what was left after they found my brother and sisters munching the forbidden ecstasy with me.

Spring

Forest budding
life in cycle
suggesting
that someone,
something,
somewhere outside
or within all of this
always
forever cares

The Collins' homestead in Counguilla, from where my mother came, was a very important part of my young world. I can remember all of my grandparents, but the longest to survive was Granny Johanna Collins. I remember two American wakes in that house. Denny was the first to follow his brother John to Oakland, California, later to be joined by his dressmaker sister Mary. I was about nine when the kitchen and dairy filled for the first wake, including their musician friends such as Pádraig O'Keeffe, Julia Clifford and Johnny O'Leary. Uncle Mike tapped the barrel with help from Tim Kenny and Tommy Fleming, the women saw to the food and Dan acted as Fear-an-Tí. Yes, the original Dan Collins, with a great fund of epic poems such as 'Dangerous Dan Magrew', and of that era in football dominated by Kerry and Kildare.

Christmas had a different feel to it then. I often speculate on the magic we would have if the innocence of the fifties could blend with the convenience of now. 'Oven ready' then meant killing and hanging your goose or turkey well in advance of the plucking and cleaning process before stuffing with a mixture of potatoes, crumbs of stale bread, and herbs. The goose was very versatile. Apart from her obvious use for the pot, her goose-grease formed the basis of many cures for pains in animals and man. Her feathers and down ensured warm slumbers in ticks and pillows long before electric blankets and central heating heralded another era. A good goose produced an amazing amount of down and feathers as they could be plucked while alive during the moulting season. Indeed I would urge today's thrill seekers to try catching and plucking a live gander without having the Red Cross on standby. Granny Collins taught me how to do it.

I remember the first time I killed a turkey in Ranaleen. I was fifteen, and thought I knew everything. We were expecting visitors. A three-year-old cock with the aggression of a gander had earned the name 'Lucifer' from the girls. Mother indicated that his big day had come. Our sisters hung back as John Joe and I caught him. The girls' initial delight that the old enemy was getting his come-uppance changed to pity when I stretched his neck across my knee and pulled until I felt a crack. Lucifer died. I tied his legs together and hung him off the rafters in the dairy. He was heavy. The girls taunted the massive limp body as it hung from the nail, wings spread helpless. About an hour later there was more excitement than at the announcement of school holidays. The resurrection of Lucifer had taken place, and the girls were screaming witnesses. He flapped those wings and hopped around the yard on bound legs. He was not pleased. Confusion and the blood in his head aggravated his fury. The second time I made absolutely sure, humble in the knowledge that my mother would have cracked his neck properly the first time.

Those days are gone; that's the way with life. But if you want to experience some of that excitement and fun you won't find it on your television set or DVD, though they are very useful in their proper place. Join with those who are doing your parish proud through their work with your local Sports Clubs, Drama Group, Macra, ICA., or Community Games. Learn to dance a polka. And don't be put off if occasionally somebody calls you a reactor.

That's only a matter of opinion. God loves a trier.

Doubting Tommy

'Twas a week before Christmas when all sorts of doubts
played around in my head like a cat with a mouse.
A girl up the road told me there was no Santy –
any a boy who believed was a bit of a pansy.

The smirk on her face told me I had been childish
To think that an ancient old saint could be flying it
With reindeer and sled and a tonnage of presents
for snotty-nosed rascals with heads full of nonsense.

In Geography class we were learning the atlas –
all the miles and the oceans from Kerry to Lapland.
Then my mind got to thinking how anyone might
find the homes of all children in one winter's night.

Yet the priest and my teachers, my father and mother
assured everyone that there truly was never
a more magical person than jolly old Santa
bringing goodness and joy like a twinkling phantom.

Could all fathers and mothers who once had been children
still believe in a fellow who is non-existent?
So I knew that thirteen-year-old girl was a bonbon
for Santa, last Christmas, had brought her a rag doll.

Teddy-Dermist

Auntie asked me to stuff the turkey while she finished knitting something. I stuffed it all right, with her favourite niece's special little Bo Bo. I had nothing against Auntie, apart from her way of asking me again and again about girlfriends. At fourteen I had only one and the girl didn't know that I had an eye for her. On the other hand my aunt had a suitable girl in mind who'd have been the perfect model for advertising toothpaste, or bath oil or anything that would make you so, so clean. Elizabeth was her name; not Liz or Betty. She was a year older and probably knew things that would have given her an advantage. And kissing her would probably be like smooching a fresh bar of soap, or a peck with the nuns at Christmas. I overheard her mother tell Auntie that her little darling was stuffing aubergines as a treat for her Granny for Christmas.

Cousin Chrissie too was older than I and, while I was around, wouldn't do any work in the kitchen. She'd do things like loosening the brakes on people's bicycles, or puncturing tyres while they were at Midnight Mass. She'd then swear she saw me doing the dirty deed. It was when she persisted in calling me 'turkey' that I thought Elizabeth's idea of a surprise for her aunt had some merit. In my imagination I saw stuffed Chrissie, or toothpaste girl, with secret ingredients like stumps of cabbage and minced snake.

Auntie made real stuffing. Hardly any potatoes; breadcrumbs had to be brown and stale; herbs went way beyond the mixture in a packet. In there you'd also find apple, banana, and whatever else gave it that texture and taste that had you wanting more while you were only half way through the first *more*. This turkey was going to be well stuffed, very well stuffed and I couldn't waste a crumb. So I took a scissors and opened Teddy's rear end in similar fashion to that of the turkey. I removed rags and bits of socks that smelled of perfumed pee and then rinsed the little fellow under a hot tap. As I squeezed it out the fabric expanded, so I decided to fit it inside the turkey and kept it in place with fists of stuffing. The rest fitted into the breast flap. I then stitched both ends up as Auntie had taught me.

To my dismay and delight, Bo Bo's owner had to be coaxed to bed without him.

'He's gone missing and will turn up,' Auntie assured her, also reminding her that a prayer to St. Anthony would surely grant her wish. That bit worried me.

On Christmas day my job was to carve the turkey, but I insisted on being a really good boy by also spooning out the stuffing. It tasted better than ever.

'It must be that wholemeal flour from the Windmill,' Auntie nodded to Chrissie as they relished yet another mouthful.

Regards, Love

Forgive me if today I wonder where you are
on this first absent Christmas. This grave gets me
as close as can for now. You're over there
maybe on that dreamed-of trip to Cassiopeia

or pondering the answers to your many questions:
how come the Holy Land is in such turmoil?
would a good God in His mercy tie a millstone
round the necks of unbelievers? Embroil

the living and the dead in a debate
about God's judgement? Is everybody really equal
in His eyes? Do human idols hold their place
on top of life's trash pyramid? You were joking.

At home they've yet to miss you from their day.
I put the turkey on before I came. Santa's been
and were you here you'd be at Mass, a while away
from grandchildren who'd each want your attention.

Sometimes you'd carve the turkey and the ham,
mull the wine, hone the carving knives or set
our two fires in the house, yet you never claimed
one role as ritual; some jobs today for eager guests.

I'll take your place at table, remember you in Grace
before and after; someone will pour the wine.
Your music in the background (they put it on a disc)
will bring a tear or smile or anecdote a while.

In their evening doze they never noticed
how you'd steal out to the kitchen, carve the remnants
of the turkey, break up the carcass for a stew pot
before I'd join you and we'd make them nibbles.

Forgive me for that smile during the funeral,
you'd have convulsed if you saw who paid obeisance.
I hope your cornucopia is brimful
and that your rest is one long happy Christmas.

Spirit Of The Abbott

Mary Dullea steered her husband to a chair beside the hearth and picked up a candle to have another look. There was no doubt; the auburn hair that had tousled in waves for thirty five years now stood in disarray on his head, whiter than the feathers she had plucked from the goose a week earlier.

'Peadar, for God's sake will you say something?'

She looked into the stare fixed in his eyes as if on a statue, and noticed that his face was different; the ginger had fled from the bristle of his beard. It too was white. His hands were clinched on something in a jute sack on his lap; the salmon he'd promised to catch for Christmas; it would stretch the goose and the bacon over the twelve days. She tried to loosen his fists but she might as well have attempted to free a stone from the arches of the bridge he had just built across the river. The usual depth of his breath gave way to a series of gasps as if he was experiencing a new fright every few seconds.

Mary wondered what on this earth could frighten a man who would defy the strongest gale to finish the eaves of a house while others huddled in awe on the ground. Though it was almost one o'clock in the morning of Christmas Eve she woke up the embers and added logs and a few sods of turf to get a fresh fire going. Then she went to the press and took out the bottle of poteen that her brother Dan Roper had brought around half past ten, when Peadar was expected home.

'Look what Dan brought us for Christmas. You'll have a drop, won't you?'

The stare in his eyes shifted. A slight movement shivered to a nod.

Mary poured a half glass and held it towards him. He looked at it as if wondering what to do next. Again she tried his fists. His right hand obeyed her urgings and clasped the glass. Soon the left hand followed.

She eased the salmon on to the floor and the glass towards his lips, blue against sallow skin that up to now had been ruddy. While praising him for surprising her with the gifts he had left in a linen sack for the children, she dipped her finger in the glass and rubbed it around his lips.

'That's it, Peadar a chroí; suck away there now. Here, take a sip from the glass yourself.'

She placed the salmon on the table, away from the fire that licked the singing kettle, and had his dinner simmering in the skillet pot once again. While she busied herself around the fire she noticed that his eyes were curious to the activity of the flames. She began to hum the lullaby he had often sung to her beside this hearth, especially earlier in their marriage. He raised the glass, looked through it at the flames and gazed as if observing the secrets of life. He took a sip.

Mary wondered what could have been worrying him to steal his youth and speech out there somewhere between morning and night. His only concern, that she had been aware of, was how he was going to provide a few Christmas surprises for the children. Where they were concerned she could always depend on him to find a way to put clothes on a promise; he had done that with some style this time. Even the linen sack, after a good bleaching, would be good enough to make a table cloth. That's why she refused her brother's offer of help, an offer made with the best intentions after a fellow tradesman broke his word to her Peadar in the finishing of their *own* house. The man charged for helping with the roof even though Peadar had earlier rebuilt the roofer's mud gables in stone to enable him to make a home out of a mud cabin, free of charge. That was not the spirit in which he'd been reared, but Peadar packed his anger into his empty pockets and built what he called a stone box for the old schoolmaster and his *old bones* committee.

She became aware of him looking at her. 'You must be starved, Peadar; hold your hour a minute and I'll have your dinner on the table.'

She held his plate in the tongs to heat over the fire before setting it on the table and emptying the skillet pot on to it. Without her asking him he moved to his place at the table, offered her the empty glass and seemed quite unaware of the aroma of the stewed rabbit and streaky bacon. She poured him a glass of milk to make things look as normal as possible, despite the hour of night, though he should be fasting for the dawn Mass.

'You got in the keystone all right, did you? On the bridge?'

He seemed to ponder her words and began to eat, ignoring the fork and picking up pieces of meat and potato and turnip with his fingers. She wondered how their children would react to this, his disregard for the fork, as if he didn't know what it was for, and the leftovers of a father the night threw back to them.

'What happened, Peadar?'

'He was there; brown, there below.' His breathing tightened again, but the terror that had swelled his eyes now became a kind of wonder.

'It can't be; no one has seen it in years.' Mary feared that her husband had seen the ghost of the hovels, perhaps even met him. The old people had often told the tale of a ghostly monk who appeared only at Christmas at either side of the old stone ditch sloping down to the river. She had never been sure whether or not to believe the story. Like most of the locals, Peadar had dismissed it as the product of heads dehydrated from poteen.

'You had a glass or two to celebrate the topping out of the bridge I suppose?' She watched a redness rising through his neck as if there was something swirling inside him trying to get out.

'One ponny of porter, and for the sake of the infant and his blessed mother will you give me another drop of that.' He looked at the bottle her brother had left. She splashed the glass and waited as he gave a sip a tour of his mouth.

'I was crossing the stile and he came from the other side in a whirlwind of a hurry, and walked through myself and the salmon as if we weren't there.'

'Maybe 'tis he wasn't there. You always said that story had no more foundation than a rainbow.'

He didn't answer, only drew his prize catch to him, took an old knife he kept specially sharpened, and cleaned and skinned the fish. While he carved it into thin slices that he would hang on the crane in the smoke of the fire, Mary again marvelled at the delicate touch in such powerful hands, even if they now trembled a little. Perhaps it was this part of him that was so susceptible to being thrown by the supernatural, she thought; the sensitive man that the stone mason wouldn't allow his belief.

She checked the blend of herbs that she would add to the stuffing, and then looked in more detail through the contents of the sack. There were books in Irish, English and Arithmetic for the three older children, and readers in both languages for the four younger ones: two woollen vests, drawers and a pair of boots for each child; a linen night-gown and a knitted cap for herself, two board puzzles, and a dozen apples that filled the kitchen with their scent. There would be no change out of a month's earnings for the lot.

While she knelt on the floor to divide the items, she recalled what she could remember about the supposed Christmas ghost and why he chose the stone wall as his patch. Her late grandfather's belief was what made her doubt the disbelief of others. He had often told of the monk Augustine Brennan who visited famine hovels, particularly at Christmas, and gave them all reason to believe that there really was a kind of God who would send his son to save those deemed by their overlords to be worthless. She would never forget how, as a child, she'd listened to him telling of the night the yoemen had captured the old Abbot in one of his acts of Christmas kindness, and summoned the people from their hovels to witness his death by being drawn apart by two horses driven in opposite directions. It had something to do with the gifts he'd given to the children being against the law, breach of which was then punishable by death or deportation.

'I see Dan brought more than the poteen this time. He must think I'm not capable of providing for my own family,' Peadar remarked as she arranged the bundles.

'But you brought these yourself, only tonight – before – don't you remember?'

She watched as he brought his hands to his head as if trying to manoeuvre his mind back into place. A fragrance like that of a summer hedgerow escaped from hiding among the apples and held Peadar as if caught in something deeper than the moment. He then filled a mug of water from the spring bucket and took it to bed.

By the time the children roused Christmas morning his hair once again coiled in a mass of curls. Tom, their eldest, worded the question for the puzzle of faces in the light of the candle.

'Your hair, Dad – the colour is gone.'

Peadar scratched his hair and looked to Mary for an explanation.

'Your dad had to help Santa after finishing the bridge, and you know the colour of his hair — from working in the frost and snow.'

That seemed to do it. The children looked at their parents and at each other and returned to the wonders of the morning. Peadar refused to go to Mass: 'at the sight of me they'd all get the fright

I got, though maybe the terror shouldn't have struck me at all,' he said as he admired the stitching on the linen sack and saw Mary and the older children off in the pony and trap.

After Mass she found old Jack Foley, the retired schoolmaster and chairman of the archeological and historical society, and asked him about any recent sightings of a ghost. He responded by urging her to tell her story. As he listened, she became aware of something like awe in his interest.

'We've always known that some of those poor people were not buried in consecrated ground, including perhaps the old Abbot himself.'

'And was his name Augustine Brennan?'

'He was Abbot of a monastery of Capuchins who were also being persecuted and, if the records are right, it's two hundred years since he was hanged, drawn and quartered.'

'And why did they kill him?'

'You were good at history if I remember rightly. Remember the Penal Laws and how education was denied to our people at the time and that anyone found speaking, reading or writing in the Irish language was as good as dead – the method was up to the executioners. But there was also the living death of the poverty in which people were trapped, depriving them of even proper clothing and footwear. So the Abbot and his monks gave themselves to the needs of the people, and suffered accordingly.' He saw the colour drain from her face as she whispered something about the Abbot still playing Santa.

'Of course your husband has built a simple tomb to contain the bones we recovered from what we believe was the execution area. We haven't been able to pay him yet but I'm sure he'll have his reward,' the old master said.

Salmon Wake

Night-poacher's prize lies fresh from the river
as dawn reveals an otter's leavings.
A salmon on the brink, a nibble

above its gills leaves it almost whole, dead
still looking alive, salt-water tired yet
offering a speckled spectrum of autumn

on a silver skin. Is it two or three
thousand miles of sense drew it back
to its birthing river bed? Lucky one

of thousands who could not sense the drifting
nets to catch their coming. So near to climax,
a cheated yearning of their need to spawn

and fertilise their future. Aloneness
must be what has left it vulnerable
to a predator that could not equal it,

but bide for shaded senses in the trust of night.
Now that he has nipped his fillet, birds wait
as wildcats prey around the feast, rip off

the skin and fins and oil each other's mittens
for a wrestle. Magpies dive and cackle,
jackdaws caw and hover in a breakfast

queue. Bills bite and pick and snap and flit for
others to partake. Still two hours to noon
black-and-white inspectors scan the carcass,

pluck out a glistening eye and then the other,
taking them as treasure for their horde.
An eyeless head, a tail following

a ribbed backbone, a raven floats and scratches
in the pebbles, appropriates the spine
and hurries off to shape it to its nest.

Sanctuary

Locals tell me it is only a ruin
in stranglehold of several-years-old
ivy, stone walls, stubborn, weathered roof
timbers once adorned by reeded thatch,
bonding long forgotten in crumbled mortar.

They do not see when *then* was *now*, are blind
to youth that lingers yet to twinkle as when
combed ashes reveal jewels of embers.
Caress of ivy here preserves a house,
a home whose hearth retains the craftsmanship

that shaped the dream. When first these trusses
snuggled under sacking, scraw and thatch, a couple,
newly wed, consummated romance
into generations for whom this abode
remained tabernacle for their hearts.

Those walls rejoiced in cries of labour pains,
of stories when each seanchaI held eyes
that would not look behind into the dark.
Wakes and weddings merge in ever-reverie.
Even without door and window the kitchen

conjures still aromas of griddle, pot
and bastible. Children born through pain
repaid that trust in pride and laughter.
Even the one poet, shaped in mystery
of wild flowers' fragrance, in time a stroll of patience,

is equal here with sibling farmer, nurse,
doctor, priest and myriad music makers.
Their spirits whisper in the ivy,
then hush in homage to a twitter
of swallows summering in the rafters.

It's In The Air

Here is our garden . . . I fancy it has grown neither better nor worse since I was a student. I don't like it. It would be far more sensible if there were tall pines and fine oaks growing here instead of sickly-looking lime-trees, yellow acacias, and skimpy pollard lilacs. The student whose state of mind is in the majority of cases created by his surroundings, ought in the place where he is studying to see facing him at every turn nothing but what is lofty, strong and elegant. . . . God preserve him from gaunt trees, broken windows, grey walls, and doors covered with torn American leather! **from A Dreary Story - Anton Chekhov**

Great literature has a way of making the village universal. Anton Chekhov believed that life is lived in ordinary moments. His countryman Leo Tolstoy, undoubtedly one of the world's greatest novelists, had the ability to set up characters and then analyse each flicker of mood as he put them through the many dimensions of the lives he gave them. Anna Karenin, though of a different social class to most who read that great novel, never fails to find common ground with the lives, personalities and emotions of those readers.

Anton Chekhov was correct in his assertion in the above quotation that students are influenced by the environment in which they study. If one lives in dull and shabby surroundings one tends to gradually become dull and shabby. Live where there's a bit of colour and life and the chances are that you'll not only pick it up but also reflect it back into the effervescence of your surroundings.

So what is so inspiring about Sliabh Luachra? How would Chekhov have regarded it? There are many landscapes more breathtaking. Turn your back on any field in the region and it will return to its natural fen at a couple of runs of the swallow. The weather is as good or dull as anywhere else in the country. In short

Earth, Fire, Water and Air reveal little of that mystery ingredient that endures in these hills, valleys, bogs and rivers.

Perhaps it's the people themselves and how history is interpreted in their genes. Let's take a brief look at that history.

Henry VIII crowned himself king of Ireland in 1541, one of the many in history who assumed that might could vanquish right. Soon he put the squeeze on local earls and chieftains, leading eventually to the broken treaty of Limerick and the rout at Kinsale. He also set out to crush the Catholic Faith, the Irish language and its associated culture and gave freedom to his armies to plunder forests, monasteries, convents and churches. A ransom of £10 was guaranteed to anyone who'd betray a priest. That was then a great deal of money, enough to set a family up in a good farm. The Dominican Fr. Thaddeus Moriarty was captured in Tralee and hanged publicly in Killarney along with Fr. Conor McCarthy of Currow. Franciscan Fr. Francis O'Sullivan managed to evade his hate-filled pursuers all the way to Scariff Island only to succumb there to the bayonet.

Such heroism does not ebb in vain. The banned language became a byword to daily living; the persecuted faith the inspiration to frustrate sword-driven laws, and sent many young women and men to convents and seminaries all over Europe. The Tyrant should have known that a great way to infuse anything with new life is to ban it. The bards and filí found themselves without patrons. Many fled overseas to Irish centres of learning such as Rome or Salamanca, some later returning as priests and teachers. Those who remained set up underground *hedge schools* and Mass rocks. One of the greatest of these was Daíbhí Ó Bruadair, a great *file* and teacher highly regarded still by many poets including the late Michael Hartnett of Newcastlewest.

The poets and writers responded in a language and idiom that could not be interpreted by the heathen invaders. It gave us the four Kerry Masters, Piaras Feiritéar of Corcha Dhuibhne, Síofra O'Donoghue of the Glens who carried on Feiritéar's work after he was hanged in 1653. Then Gneeveguilla gave us the great Aodhagán O'Rathaille (1675–1728) followed by the abundantly talented rascal Eoghan Rua Ó'Súilleabháin (1748 –1784), the Dylan Thomas of his time. Both were classical scholars but as opposite in personality and outlook as one could get.

A century later that hinterland gave us the poet Ned Buckley and that most eminent Lexicographer Fr. Patrick Stephen Dinneen, author and co-author of many works, but most famous for his Irish / English Dictionary. The legacy of Aodhagán and Eoghan Rua has increased and multiplied into the present not just in the Tolstoy-like attention to nuance and detail in the storytelling of the late Eamon Kelly, in Bernard O'Donoghue – one of the most accomplished poets in any land, in poets writing in Irish such as Dónal Ó'Síocháin, in Marion Moynihan, Karen O'Connor and Eileen Sheehan, whose poetry is acclaimed and enjoyed all over the land and poet/translator Eugene O'Connell who already has a well-deserved national and international profile, but also in the songwriters and musicians, storytellers, historians and dancers who cherish and enhance their heritage. They have emerged from the wild womb of Sliabh Luachra and endowed it with a mystical and mythical ethos in Irish and World Folklore.

Anton Chekhov would surely be impressed.

Long Dusk

for an Irish emigrant in California, 1953

As I try to get my legs
accustomed to a street-walk stride,
watch traffic, don't walk, walk, drag
myself to another building site
too tired from trying to side step
something in my head ransacking
explanations that won't bridge the gap
from Scartaglen to San Francisco,

I wonder if my dream is naked.
The gold that I thought waited here
must have tired and tried instead
to notion a new reverie.
Not everything I miss is missing
me: a quarter tierce of Irish stout;
a meal of bacon, praties, cabbage
in the bog as we'd recount

the deeds of other generations,
those who gave their lives as ransom
so that we might have a nation,
sunsets as evening gilded dusk to charm
night – out here does not need seduction.
Our day surrenders without time
to pipe a post, or even to intone
a Vespers before last Compline

To shovel anger through this concrete funnel
and earn more bonus pay while day allows
might get me in the slipstream of that seagull
to rescue future dreams from early shroud.

Cupid's Morsel

If you could sing you'd versify a maid
pressing wild daisies beside a river
in the summer of her love, like the days
and nights when Eros taught me to regale
my lover with the berries of a briar.
Not even Epicure's long-life champagne
could frolic on the taste buds or compare
with this ambrosial dark Guinness brew
swirling to the call in a tulip jar.

Aperitif, or course that once was porter,
stokes those memories that linger on my tongue
like the nectared kisses new-shucked oysters
bring to mind as we, lovers ever young,
feed each other once-upon-a-time fresh
promises of Eden, foreplay prolonged
in lips and fingertips of whispered touch.

We relive nights when the moon played striptease
with see-through wisps of cloud, reprising each
of Aphrodite's dreams, a Paradise
of *His* and *Hers*, two worlds ringed forever,
seducer and seduced epitomised
in inner eyes that ponder life and wonder
if somehow, to still the Creator's wrath,
you offered yourself up whencesoever
to propagate the precept, Go *you forth,*
increase and multiply throughout the Earth.

Preface – Field Work

Working the fields can be hard but it has its rewards. You feel that
liaison with nature as you prepare the ground for the seeds and
then cheat the weeds so that the seeds bloom to harvest. You
always have something to show for your work as sunset sends
each day to rest.

As each day of spring grows into summer and summer ripens to
autumn people gather in meitheals to help each other to harvest
their crops. With the harvest secure for another winter, people
congregate in the rambling houses to celebrate with stories of
other harvests and harvesters, to sing, dance and rejoice in an
intimacy that stimulates other fertility.

Spade and Ladle

Children through the kitchen door offer season's
wild pickings: strawberries, crab apples, blackberries,
mushrooms, herbs I've shown them in the ditches.

Husband in the kitchen lays out organic freshness:
roots, brassica, fruits of thoughtful spade.
I cook this potage to a bouquet summons to my ladle.

Sun and breeze dance on cornfield sheen
and harvesting tunes up production lines where we work
to extract juices from the freshness and package seasons ready
any time.

Just add water, and that is at its best
springing out of timeless calcium rock, and bottled now for taste.

Children through the kitchen door, husband in the kitchen.
Home-cooked food is at its best when your heart is in it.

Story Root

The boy and girl return
to the orchard of their Granddad's memory,
their tap root to the family tree.
Young again, he recalls stories
of his grandmothers and grandfathers,
about their ways of living
when life expected little
but became adventure when lived for
                                    each other.

He tells them of the woman, Sarah,
left with her daughter and fifteen cows
after the Flight of Earls,
and how, in harbouring their stock,
mother and daughter became sister
warriors, feared by those who would
                        rustle cow, or calf or bull.

He tells the story of the time they trailed
a pair of stolen heifer calves
and brought them back in Chieftain's horse
and chariot which they, in honour, kept;
and later how they rode the chariot
to Grainne's wedding when she took
the hand of Chieftain's son in marriage
                        and gave two heifers as her dowry.

They watch their Granddad scan horizons
joining distant skies to landscape,
imagining the warrior women
Sarah and her daughter Grainne
in their family tree. He sits
in his bench in shade of apple branches.
They see his searching frown as he tries
                        to grip the width of history.

He listens as the auburn grandson
whispers to his flaxen sister
that their questions may be loading
too much on ancient whitened head.
He smiles, they take his outstretched arms
and help him upright. Joined together
as they walk, he says the tree has no one
place for their women warrior forebears,
their sap rises in each limb and leaf
                        and blossom.

Ellis Island Ferry

The usher Apple-chats us into line,
tourists on a trip to history.
No need to be afraid of me because I'm black,
underneath I'm just like you or you,
he laughs as he removes his vest
and somersaults along
the outside of the barricade.

He works our eyes along the ripples of his
pose as, behind his back,
another black and white tune up guitar and mike.
The singer leads familiar lyrics
Day-o, day-o, daylight gone an' I wanna leave home,
tinted with the antics of his humour.
Two acrobats leap like sharks
to urge us close together.

A guffaw from down the queue
draws our singer like a boy scout to a spark,
coaxing sniggers to a flicker, then a flame.
Another fifteen minutes your ferry will be back
to dock its load before you get aboard,
we're told, as a glow
synergises through our faces.

All we want is for y'all to be happy,
the performing faces smile again.
As the ferry is being docked
our singer smiles alone
and his colleagues offer
the facility of hats
where we can tip
our dollars.

Later,
after touching lives of exiles
through the point of immigration,
our voyage returns by the statue
lighting Liberty for Peoples:
another group is corralled in bemusement;
strangers being de-iced into a party.

Fertility

Steel of plough or spade earths the seeds
in nests of dung, they die in giving birth.
Triplets, quads, shoots galore surge for spring
in league with hoof and wing in country air.

Roots, tubers snuggle deep in fertile mother,
craving space, they stretch her belly thin.
Again steel drives in to furrow,
raising earth to feed and clothe new life.

Sun and rain encourage greening plumes
as breezes carry scented progress
to alert farmer's senses. Disease
may threaten ripening but will die

at hands of jealous husband of the soil.
Ripe, ready excitation crackles.
Days mowing, digging, flailing, threshing,
barns assemble nature's cycle.

Another harvest, time to cherish
guests, new friends to join with old
as people gather, goatskin rhythm dances
into music of the marrow.

Tradition coaxes limbs to youthful zest
commemorating yesterdays when crops
perished in the womb, casting people out
to sow and grow their seeds in other lands.

Him Eye Alive

'We feel him over, see all him bits be joined up,' Mop and Top McCarthy agree as they crouch over the prone body of a Palomino foal.

From a nearby cliff top the twins have seen it before it happens. Like an egg on crown of head; sure to tumble, only when, they nodded. They kicked ashes over the embers of the last of their father's things, climbed down to the beach and ran across to the base of the other cliff. To get there by road would take an age without a bike or pony. A flowing tide got there before them. Though small for their thirteen years they knew how to ride these waves, and soon flung themselves out of the swirl on to the lower rocks. They shivered in the grey morning.

The water was not yet deep enough to break the fall where they feared the foal might land. They worked their way around to those jagged rocks. More than two hundred feet above them the plateau of the cliff top dipped suddenly. The danger was that the gambolling foal would run too quickly into this hollow and lose his balance.

To the consternation of those who did not know them they had often climbed the rocky faces of these cliffs as children. Barefooted, they had learned to cling to those rocks like moss and lichen. For the past two years however, they'd spent most of their free time helping their father in his harness-making and repairs business, and accompanying him to horse fairs and markets. They found this even more fun than swimming and climbing. It was miles better than school when Pops and Molly showed them all about leather, how to draw patterns, and the different ways of waxing, cutting and stitching. Then the fun of learning to read the eyes and faces of would-be customers, to be able to tell chancer from buyer by the feeling at the back of your eye. During that time the yew slip growing from the ledge fifty feet from the top had become a sturdy little tree. This, they hoped, could break the fall of the giddy foal, if he didn't fall in too much of a hurry.

They climbed to a ledge above the tide mark and hid their boots there. Beneath them they heard the roar and gurgle of surf rushing and ebbing through the caves. They touched hands in a good-luck wish and began to scale the cliff face. Out of habit, Top took his place to the left and a little ahead of Mop. Soon their fingers and toes recognised those little grooves and cracks they'd so often gripped. Something was different, however.

'More moss now,' Top remarked.

'And we not so small,' Mop added as they paused almost half way up. This was the point from where the cliff went straight up for twenty feet. Until now Top would climb on to Mop's shoulders and get a grip. Mop would then haul himself up over Top and find his hold. Eight, or so, repetitions of this manoeuvre would get them to an alcove where they'd often rest and look at the horror on people's faces as they pointed and called up at them from the beach.

'Keep eye on boys, Pops,' Mop prayed as he took a hold and beckoned Top to pull himself up.

'Fingers hard but toes bit soft,' Top grunted as he climbed.

A few curious gulls flew over and hovered. The boys found their old rhythm and strove for the alcove. The gulls called out. Soon they were joined by hundreds more, along with curlews and a swarm of starlings. Top's fingers found a familiar groove in the alcove. He tightened his grip and squeezed his arms against his ears to block out the screeching wail that surrounded them. Mop climbed over him and pulled him up on to the narrow ridge.

'They go soon,' Mop said as he held his brother and stroked his head.   Top pressed his hands against his ears and did not try to stop his tears. It was like the night their father had been killed: Top's panic at the sound of gunshot; the screaming women and children; Mop rushing to where his father lay on the ground and catching his last words – 'Mistake - accident - no revenge - no revenge - Molly - Molly.' Then a gurgle, a kind of croak and his eyes stopping still, dead still, seeing no more.

A cormorant, unmoved by the flapping din, perched on a fern stump above their heads, standing guard like a customs officer waiting to check their passports. The birds, seeing no more action from the boys than from the surrounding rock, lost interest and flew away. Top took his hands from his ears and clung to Mop like he had done for so many nights in their bunk after their father's funeral. Today they'd hoped that carrying out the tradition of making a fire of the things of their dead would burn their sadness into smoke and their pain to hope.

When their tears trickled away they wiped their faces on each other's shoulders. With one mind they turned their eyes on their home, one of ten cottages around a common area with a grassy rood in the middle. Theirs was different because their father had built a mobile home in the tiny back yard. Even though it could never go anywhere it held a different feeling to the cottage; going to bed there always put wings on their dreams.

Top stiffened. 'Foal – run wild,' he said. Mop didn't hear the gallop, but trusted his brother's ears. 'That boy could hear a filly blink,' Molly, their mother, had often joked. A tumbling whinny, then the foal found itself wedged at the base of the yew tree thirty feet above them. Mop gave Top a leg-up, and they scrambled together to the tree. Though the foal was tiny they dragged it back as far as possible lest the young tree lose its grip.

      *   *   *

Top places his head against the foal's ribs and listens. 'No heart; I hear no thrum-a-bop,' he whispers.

Mop lifts an eyelid and blows a soft breath into the eye. 'Him eye alive,' he says.

'Alive? How alive no blink?' Top asks as he jabs the foal in the chest and ribs as if this was one of his pretend games with himself as doctor or sheriff and Mop as patient or outlaw. He jabs and pushes, then listens again. They change the foal's position to allow them to simulate breathing movement as they press on and release his ribs.

'No please; no, no, no!' Top yells to the top of the cliff. 'He mother go crazy up there; she fall down here too, down and kill us all,' Top's eyes are on fire.

'Him down here; you foal with boys, all right,' Mop adds.

Water, lots of icy water, the boys think; a splash would surely snap this whippet of a foal out of shock and get it started again. Immediately they think better of it because if the foal were to revive and try to escape it would tumble to a great splash indeed. But they would have to get breath happening, otherwise death would have the last word. Top lifts an eyelid and breathes in there as he's seen Mop do. He looks at the eye and watches the way Mop looks it over.

'How you know he eye alive?'

'How you know him mother go crazy?' Mop shrugs. Immediately a thought hits them. 'Okay, I whisper things in ear and you rub up heart,' Top nods and points up again at the racket on the cliff top. Mop is already massaging where he knows the foal's heart to be, little circles getting bigger and back to little again.

'What I say to him?' Top asks.

'What you like him say to you if you in big shock.'

Top's whispers trickle like the waters of a stream. His fingers play around the foal's ears and down between his eyes. Bet no one thought of a name for you, Mop thinks as he watches his twin, and then realises the name he should have. He wonders if Top feels the same. If Top chooses the same name then it is meant to be.

'What you think for him name?' Mop asks.

'Pops' name surely; same as you feel,' Top nods.

'Okay, little foal, you name be Pablo,' the boys tell him.

'You mom up there be real worried, Pablo,' Top continues, 'maybe think you even dead. Silly boy, you no dead, Mop know you eye alive and if any teeny weeny bit of you alive you be okay. You no pretend dead now, little Pablo? You mom no know what to do, and you dad be in stable somewhere, I suppose. Our dad be real dead. Maybe he bit silly too, like you running into danger hollow no knowing it be dangerous. People come in camp with gun after someone they no like. Guns real bad, cold bad, kill so fast you eye be dead before sound of gun leave you ear. Bad purple-red sound rip through head, like bullet go in there and burst. And our dad try talk to mad bad men. He tell them about our camp full of no trouble, never no trouble in our camp, Little Pablo. Our dad be man folks in all our camps want to do talk. All time when Pops stand up and talk to trouble it just crumble like sand castle or go away. But bad man mad angry so he shoot anyways. Gun shake in he hand like it be hot out of fire, so he miss man but – oh. One shot – and other bad man grab gun, but bullet hit Pops where Mop rubbing you now. Pops fall on he knees, holding he chest, like he pray. Bang blast in my ears, try get out but can't. Pops topple but Mop run and catch head, hold head to heself and listen. He hear words of real good man. I hear too.'

Top stops. 'You hear that?' he says, and listens.

'Hear what?' Mop asks.

'He blood. He blood run again.'

'Holy smoke, you keep whisper him ear and hold him head down.'

'But he okay now?'

'He no okay if he get jumpy,' Mop says as he begins to check on each of the four legs. He asks Top to stand back so that they can both observe him.

'You no happy?' Top asks.

'Might be something with him back; he no trying to move.'

'He blinking now, see.'

'Should be trying get up, though.' Just then the foal breaks wind and everything kicks and jerks. 'Hold him head down; I go get help,' Mop says.

'No, no; you better with him. I go,' Top says and does not wait for argument.

Mop takes hold of Pablo's head with one hand and puts his fingers in the foal's mouth. The foal immediately begins to suck.

'You get no milk out of there but won't be for want of trying, little foal,' Mop smiles. For a moment he thinks he could get under the foal and try to scramble to the top, piggy back style. Just as quickly he throws the idea away. It's one thing to face into a cliff with a brother who knows your every move and gets as close to the rocks as feathers on a bird; it just wouldn't work with a foal that is still learning what his bits and pieces are for.

He looks across at their cottage. A man seems to be talking to Molly outside the house, talking at her, it looks more like. If Top was here he could make out what they're saying. The man is trying to get her to take something. Molly's hands are saying 'no'. No sign of Julie; neighbours nowhere. Then the hairs stand up on his body; that icy-lice feeling worms in and out of his skin. That man Molly is pushing away is the one that shot Pops. Mop should be there but has to be here. Maybe Top hear and fly across. Foal not feeling happy neither, but at least he feeling. Want legs under him, make little knobs of dung.

Julie there now, shouting something, showing man mobile phone. Molly do her kick, man on ground holding him crotch. Neighbours there now, maybe telling bad man to count him luck. Julie run in house and come out with horse shoe; hold in fist and stand over man. He get in van.

Mop hears his name from a big coil of rope up at the cliff top. Top is back with curious help. Half the village dogs stand at the edge, look down and try a few steps. They realise they're not cats so they step back and bark. Gulls hover. Top shoos them, asks them please be quiet. The mare also takes a look. Grey cloud cover reveals the spot where the sun is trying to burn through.

'Old fire brigade rope; help here soon,' Top calls down.

'Tie end around something, then toss over.'

Top takes a look and secures the end of the rope round the base of a bush, tosses the coil towards Mop and climbs down. He loves the bit where he can bounce off the cliff face like a mountain climber. By the time he lands on the ledge Mop has the end shaped into something like a cat's cradle, only bigger. The foal's legs secure each corner.

'We get you momma to pull you up, you and me,' Mop says. Pablo tries to stand and join in their enthusiasm. Mop calms him as Top climbs back up.

The mare prances around him as he unties the rope from the bush. He loops it around her neck and knots it so that it will not run. He advises Mop of this.

'Has she halter?' Mop asks. Top affirms that she has one of real leather; the pony seems to be showing it off. He notices that her hooves are pared. A closer look shows that she's freshly shod. Obviously someone thinks a great deal of this mare.

'Okay up here,' he says.

'Line her up to steeple and walk, nice and slow,' Mop calls. Top and the mare obey. 'Mop make cradle for you little Pablo and we pull them up together; no straight up, that be danger too much even for Mop,' he tells the little mare what's happening. She struggles and strains against the rope. You better than any 4 x 4, Top encourages her, telling her how far more they have to go: forty, thirty, twenty feet; the mare is panting for breath, fifteen, ten. People begin to arrive. The mare doesn't seem to like this. Top signs them to be quiet and points to the rope creeping slowly over the cliff edge.

They see a foal plop on to the plateau. It is tiny, the colour of light coffee gilded with cream. The mare turns and drags Top to the scene. Mop crawls out from under Pablo and begins to undo the cradle. The mare licks her foal as if he's just been born. Pablo raises his head. Mop helps him to stand and re-introduces him to his mother's udder. He removes the belt from his trousers and ties it around the foal's neck. Top puts his shirt back on and coils the rope into a circle on the ground as the fire brigade arrives.

'We go home now,' Top suggests. Mop shakes his head, holds on to Pablo and will not let him go. Pablo tries another taste of fingers.

'No leave Pablo here; him tumble over again,' he protests.

The fire brigade members look at the scene and at each other, then pick up the rope and leave. Killer-man arrives in his van, winds down the window and calls to the boys.

'Run; he kill us,' Top starts to run.

'Back. Think,' Mop calls. 'Cool, man. Hard. Play pretend hard man, okay?'

Top places his hands on his hips, and nods.

'Leave him eff off,' Mop shouts. With one mind they walk with Pablo around towards Pops' embers. The mare follows.

'You like Palomino?' Killer-man calls after them.

The boys slow down and look at each other. 'What would Pops do in a case like this?' is the unworded question between them. Killer-man crawls out of the van. He is bent over, not like when his gun killed Pops. He beckons, and scrambles after them.

'You like, you keep,' Killer-man pants.

'These two yours?'

'Yours now, life for life. Never meant no harm to your father.'

Top spits at Killer-man's feet. Mop pulls him aside for a whisper about accepting anything from Killer-man with their father's blood on it.

'Pablo no yours, we save him life,' Mop says.

'Pony then; like sacrifice, for what I done.'

'You sorry, mister?' Top asks.

'You have to believe me, I swear.'

The twins and Pablo watch as tears well in Killer-man's eyes.

'She be the world to me. Ten years I trade pony for foals, then I trade two ponies for Palomino filly.' He holds trembling hands towards them. There's an envelope in the hand that held the gun. 'You be too young of understanding, but it be that hairy good-for-nothing Bubba I wanted to – to frighten; no kill, never kill. Got inside my woman's head so he did; now she be all Bubba this, Bubba that, and everyone they laugh at me.'

'What name you give her, mister?' Mop asks.

'The pony? Gertie, same as my own mother.' He signs a cross on his chest.

'Maybe you best be away, mister,' Top says.

'Them be real true-bred Palomino, these be them papers for mare and foal,' Killer man offers the envelope towards them. His mouth continues to shape words but he cannot find sound for even a syllable.

The boys observe. They know what the next move must be and are about to make it when the man spits in his other hand and takes a step closer, holding it towards them as if offering them birthday cake from Heaven's oven.

The boys cross hands. Mop spits in Top's and Top in Mop's. Then they move to the man and smack their spit on to his. He knots his fingers around their hands and slobbers a kiss all over their wrists.

'These be all of every bit of me in world, 'cept for that there old van an' my Bubba-fool woman,' he croaks and holds the envelope tied in twine towards them.

'Just leave it there on ground, mister,' Mop says.

Pablo nibbles at the envelope as the man hobbles away.

Clan File literally means ***Poet to the Clan***

Its genealogy predates Christianity back into the Bardic tradition.
Their centres of learning included poetic schools centred around
a Chief Bard of Fileóir Ollamh, where poets and other students
served a seven-year training period. The Clan File is expected to
eulogise the clan and to satirise with caution.

Chieftain
(In memory of Cornelius Mountiford Conner,
Prince Chieftain of The O'Connor Kerry Clan, 1992 - 2001)

He answered the call in Nineteen Ninety Two
as bloodline Prince Chieftain O'Connor;
a Clan scattered far by turmoil, renewed
Craobh Rua's tradition and honour.

In history's hide-out Con saw no taboos
when the flame of his candle awakened
a heritage waiting its time to accrue
and the past with the present be blended.

Cornelius Mountiford Conner,
a scholar whose vision of life was that all
would live better if working together,
as people at peace in the lessons of war.

Far beyond Ballineen his life resonates,
deep as the Bandon, the colour of candour;
Prince Chieftain Conner ascends to that place
where a man for his time is ennobled.

Misneach Chiarraí

(Anthem for the O'Connor Kerry Clan – July 2001,
arranged for pipe music composed by Danny Houlihan)

I

The Kings and Chieftains of Ciarraí Luachra
are testament to the line of Ciar,
a people honed in unyielding battle,
history's witness will persevere.

Refrain   Let us muster, as a ring fort,
          to guard and cherish our *Oidhreacht*;
          in words and deeds our heritage lives
          and thrives on the way to tomorrow.
          In words and deeds our heritage lives
          and thrives on the way to tomorrow.

II

No sword can ravage resourceful spirit,
or traitor hope for our final grave;
today no boundary sets a limit,
our future reborn in every age.

Refrain   Let us muster, as a ring fort,
          to guard and cherish our *Oidhreacht*;
          in words and deeds our heritage lives
          and thrives on the way to tomorrow.
          In words and deeds our heritage lives
          and thrives on the way to tomorrow.

III

The shell and canon that breach a castle
rust in time avaricious deeds.
our Ciarraí Kingdom has rock foundations,
bravery's spirit flourishes here.

Refrain   Let us muster, as a ring fort,
            to guard and cherish our Oidhreacht;
            in words and deeds our heritage lives
            and thrives on the way to tomorrow.
            In words and deeds our heritage lives
            and thrives on the way to tomorrow.

IV

From Shannon waves to the Kenmare River,
Blasket Sound back to Scartaglin,
on Skellig Michael and Tarbert Island
legend renews again and again.

Refrain   Let us muster, as a ring fort,
            to guard and cherish our *Oidhreacht;*
            in words and deeds our heritage lives
            and thrives on the way to tomorrow.
            In words and deeds our heritage lives
            and thrives on the way to tomorrow.

V

May God look kindly on generations
past and present and yet unborn;
give fortitude so we'll join together
always willing to share and learn.

Refrain Let us muster, as a ring fort,
           to guard and cherish our *Oidhreacht*;
           in words and deeds our heritage lives
           and thrives on the way to tomorrow.
           In words and deeds our heritage lives
           and thrives on the way to tomorrow.

*Misneach = Irish word incorporating Courage.
*Oidhreacht = Irish word meaning Inheritance.

Carraigafoyle

Defiant castle at Carrigafoyle,
the eye of the Shannon in times of war
defaced by the hanker of shell and ball,
shows how to stand in the face of turmoil.
The Kerry fortress still bears many scars
of foreign invaders who thought that force
would end the stronghold of clan concourse.
Could those bombarding the quarry-stone walls
believe they could breach a bond reinforced
by each-for-each-other through fire and hate?
Allow them to claim the right to dictate
the life or death of a dynasty source?
Carrig refuses to be a ruin,
its pride a progeny strong as the lion.

Sliabh Luachra haiku

(Acer Palmatum)
a young Japanese maple probes outside its cage

a Labrador sniffs for maybes in the deadwood

seated on that rock the tramp is king

forever child too big now for the swings happy on the roundabout

the elm without its top still believes

a stiff steel crane stands above the treetops

a bird-watching party listens through the years of the old master

birds in chorus make the park a cathedral

a little hillock pushes up trees so it seems taller

the sun writes trees on the grass
no translation needed

Whose Is She?

I cannot be sure but I feel it's a *she*,
the hare looking at me
up on its hind legs for a better view;
or perhaps to wonder what I am
doing here, or not doing,
not nibbling grass,
not twitching my nose.

To the harmony of scent that meanders
in the breeze, she rambles to heartbeat rhythm
while my eyes follow through a break of briars,
clumps of rushes, reeds in their take-or-leave demeanour
as if a hare playing hide-and-seek
(with yet another geek)
is a moment hardly worth a look.

Who is observing whom?
Whose place, whose home is this?
Whose hare is this?

Alive she may be some buck's wife
or may have chosen her mate
from the many who figured
that being equipped with a semen kit
would win another maiden.

On hind legs again, front paws open to the view,
her gaze suggests the answer:
here in her own place she belongs
to no one.
She is with here.

Free Green

I contemplate a fragrant summer truth:
daisies, buttercups, dandelions free
in grass that at this time should be as smooth
as a green carpet, where that honey bee
meanders in the nectared joy of youth.
What kind of garden was Gethsemane?
Is there a freedom cavorting here that
had to wait my thoughts for habitat?

I must decide if what I always thought
about a garden, everything in place,
clean-edged, weedless, pruned, always as it ought
to be, unless it would be a disgrace.
Ideal gardens now seem overwrought,
sprayed, clipped and irrigated to embrace
those magazine impressions without flaw,
forbidding cat or dog to place a paw.

Your garden's looking well, the neighbours say,
or, *You'll be doing that garden soon*, they hint.
But as I sit and watch the children play
in foliage and grasses of a length
that spells the happiness in disarray,
I'm not alarmed at seeing the odd footprint
that gives a lived-in look, without rebukes;
and my garden feels better than it looks.

When The Time Is Right

Liam is my wife's favourite neighbour. He likes being listened to, especially the way Judith entertains every word of his latest gripe. A surveyor in her father's architectural practice, he set the levels for our patio last summer and then arranged delivery of the gravel, sand and stone. Apart from insisting on selecting the stone, all I had to do was pay the bill and shut my hearing to his derision of my selection.

The patio has been waiting for twenty-one months and I've decided that I have to lay it tomorrow.

'But Liam says it'll take three days, maybe more with those crazy stones,' she says.

'I'm doing it tomorrow, on my own.'

The way I rejected Liam's offers of help to lay down what had formed in my mind did not meet with her approval. Allowing him anywhere near my plan would mean handing it over to him, giving him further opportunity to show off to Judith, while I would end up with a replica of symmetrical perfection like his own patio, or the one he had laid for Judith's father. And he would again regale his friends in the club with the tendencies of my DIY towards, what he regarded as, catastrophe. She must understand what I'm like when an idea forms inside me and then enslaves me until I give it expression.

Thankfully it is such a different world in the Gallery: canvas, linen, oils, enamel, parchment; three-dimensional things with the calming scent of centuries. I work on the paintings, maintaining a proper environment, alert for signs of stress, re-touching where necessary: hanging exhibitions in themes.

That was how I first met Judith, seven years ago. I'm not likely to forget that meeting, though I'm not good on the detail of times and dates.

I had become temporarily famous for finding a Monet – ALICE – hidden under a naturalistic landscape in pieces donated from private collections. I was thirty, single. A similar discovery three years earlier had me sharing headlines with the CAMILLE. I couldn't explain exactly how I had known, so media people labelled me psychic. Some even gave me X-ray eyes. I was a curiosity, for a while.

What really happened was that both paintings created hell with the soul or spirit who shares my mind. Yes, they bore the authentic signature of Claude Oscar Monet. They still showed some of his brush strokes even though someone had decided that the works were unfinished; and filled them in. Absolutely finished them, almost.

It was as if I had allowed Liam to complete my patio in ordinary perfection, only worse. I pointed out the near perfect merging of colour, the imposition of weakness on strength. The originals must have felt like powerful swimmers being overpowered by an oil slick.

The fact that I could restore – CAMILLE AND THE LILLIES – to what Claude had visualised won me permission to prove my theory in the studio. It helped that somehow I recognised those parts of the original untouched. I felt the line of the strokes suffocating beneath the added paint; Naturalistic mediocrity imposed on Impressionistic mastery.

CAMILLE took her place in evening light, brushed to timeless-ness in mutual love. So when the ALICE manifested herself to me I became the subject of a documentary. I had to agree to comment on the detailed stages of restoration, on video. Because of the nature of the work, I made my commentary in English and French. After all, the originals had been conceived and painted in French.

Invitations to parties became a feature of my post. On those occasions I was expected to expound on the works of the Masters, with particular emphasis on any scandal in their lives. Judith's father had a private Renoir collection, and requested an evalua-tion. Twelve pieces, unquestionably Pierre Aguste Renoir, hung in strategic locations in the reception rooms; one in some difficulty from exposure to direct sunlight and dust attracted by electricity in the over-polished frame. I explained that it would be possible to restore it, and promptly received a generous commission to undertake the work provided that I did not remove the painting from his premises.

Outside in his acre of garden he had a pond, which he called a lake, formed by a diversion from a brook into the grounds and back out through a concealed sluice. It was Judith who introduced me to it, and to the possibilities of herself standing beside it. I allowed her chatty comments to flow as I restored Renoir's work to its original texture and hung it in a place that could have been set for it in another part of the hallway.

She asked me to paint her by the pond; only, like her father, she called it a lake. It was as if she had caught some of my compulsion. I hesitated in deference to that other part of me, and then relented to her urgings. Monet would have been proud of the finished work. Judith certainly was.

'You've just made me live forever,' she said.

'Thanks. You flatter me.' I waited for her to say something to help me interpret the message in her eyes as they flickered over me between glances at the finished canvas.

'I'm sure you've things to do — hobbies and so on?' My question was by way of a prompt, to remind her that she was free to get on with whatever she would normally be doing at this time.

'Hobbies? Well, I like the idea of being taken out to dinner by famous people.'

I relaxed, confident that I was disqualified.

A quizzical frown, a tilt of that regal head, suggested —

'such as you, for instance.'

'You'd like to come to dinner with me?' I could not hide my dismay.

'You're so very kind. Thursday, about seven perhaps. How does that sound?'

'Should be very interesting.' After a while observing the breeze in her hair and how well she wore that floral dress, I added: 'you look beautiful, against the pond; pity there weren't lilies.'

'Pond? Don't let Dad hear you call it that. It's a lake; very special. He built it himself, and don't you forget it.'

The waiter offered me the wine to taste. At the table she savoured her own food and portions of mine which I didn't get to on time, making it seem like she was helping me out.

'You don't often take ladies out to dinner, do you?'

'No.'

'So I thought. Never, I'd guess?' She spooned a baked potato on to my plate. I nodded. As the meal progressed I was happy that her words and opinions confirmed my earlier impression.

'You're probably too busy with your art to have a regular lady friend,' she observed as dessert arrived. She shrugged a reply out of me with a smile.

'What do you think of courtship anyway?' She picked a grape out of my fresh fruit cocktail. I wanted to tell her that it seemed crude when compared to what one could do with a brush; time consuming without any guarantee of progress.

'I can't claim any experience; I've never really had the time,' I said.

'Exactly as I thought. Exactly.' She leaned across the table, searching my eyes as if to read what I was thinking. Her face had a curious beauty. I tried to keep my eyes out of her sun-tanned cleavage.

'I think we should marry.' She waited until I finished coughing into my napkin. 'You need a wife, and I cannot see you courting anybody, except me, through your magnificent brushes. And you obviously love me.' She raised the empty bottle out of the ice-bucket to remind me to re-order. 'In fact if you were to ask me now, here where you look so right against the dark oak, I'd accept.'

'Would you, really?'

'Oh, my precious, there's no need to ask. I'd love to be wife to you.'

'But we barely know each other.' My mouth was still open but the next words were delayed somewhere.

'You're saying you don't know me! So how come you've painted me from the inside out?' She offered me her raised glass. 'To us,' she said. We touched.

Liam was best man at our wedding. Soon he was our best friend, and then ...

Anyway, back to the patio.

'Don't you think I should get Liam to help? You know he wants to. And you're bound to come up with something way out.'

'I know what I'm doing,' I insist.

'Why can't you be normal and sociable? Sometimes, I don't know... it's as if you've mislaid your head and put on someone else's by mistake.'

The area is five metres long and four wide, Liam's perfect rectangle. But I see an ellipse. I spread the gravel to the levels. Soon it will settle under the weight of the stones and my weight as I work on them and coax them into position.

There's something about Judith; not resting, giddy almost. I wonder if it's the delay with the patio, or maybe it's about starting a family; I haven't suggested it since she threw my own words back at me about the delay with the patio. 'When the time is right,' I'd promised. There was very little promise in the spin Judith put on the same words last night.

There isn't a regular size of stone in the heap; mostly small sizes in colours from yellow through green, brown, black, dark blue, speckled and streaked. I bind some in on edge, cobblestone style. They'll provide a brace for their neighbours laid flat. I toss the stones on to the gravel bed, mixing colour almost at random. But the pattern in my head comes alive on the bed. Stones snuggle together as if they've been shaped for each other. I re-check the surface levels with the straight edge, edges now reaching their fingers into the neighbouring soil, the soil taking each stone and giving of itself. Earth and stone tuck into the firm feel of each other, naturally.

I spread bonding sand over my work, teasing it into the joints. Judith is at the end of the garden among the sunflowers. I try not to feel her lack of faith in my work. Colour swirls in the stone. Stone becomes a living thing like the paintings in the gallery. Two women, Camille and Alice in the somewhere. Grey in the centre blending into speckled pieces holding brown and greens to themselves. Why is she carrying an 'if' in her head about conceiving our baby?

Liam is leaning over the fence, talking to her. No 'if's' in me as my patio defines itself; altogether stating something other than the combination of its parts, pieces of stone important to each other.

Conversation murmurs. They look towards my work. Dark pieces on the outside embrace the centre as I trowel and brush in the finishing sand; weak sand becoming strong in the grip of the grooves.

He's over the fence. They approach, Liam a half-step ahead. I stand barefooted in the middle of my mosaic, close my eyes and await the approval of touch. Inch by inch I move around the centre. Grains of sand play with my toes. The stones that had waited in a pile now want the feel of my skin. They do not waver in their embrace.

Liam and Judith are behind me. Whispers fade into the hush.

'We have something to tell you,' a voice quivers. I do not respond.

'We agreed you should be the one to tell him, Judith.'

A chill chases from my toes up through my skin.

'Oh, darling, it's — now I see what you've been trying to say,' she says.

'I can't make anything of it.' Liam contradicts her.

'I was speaking to my husband,' she says.

Fusion

On the occasion of the marriage of my sister Monica to Danny O'Keeffe.

20th March 2005

Sense of expectancy
like the aroma of apples drizzled in honey
and baked in a pie.

Scent of wood shavings as what was once a tree takes on another
life;
first in the maker's eye,
then in obedience to the trade in his hands.

Shinnagh, Cnoc na Locha – Danny in the noble trade of Joseph
plied in a sanctuary for the animal that bore Mary to Bethlehem
and Jesus into Jerusalem on the feast we celebrate today.

Ranaleen, Caherbreagh, Oileán Chiarraí, Abbeyfeale —
Monica, baby of ten and like Brigid in the care she shares
with those who've come to know
and trust her knowledge.

Shinnagh, Cnoc na Locha,
Ranaleen, Caherbreagh —
giving love new life on the hill of Doneen.

Mosaic of life in continuous change
welcomes a new family into its alloy,
blending unique DNA into the interlace.

Love: that emotion without bounds
takes a lifetime to learn, to grow,
and flourishes beyond time;
expressed in many ways,

it grows and comes to know
the many other things two can do in a room;
it can be a diamond,

a single exquisite rose
or a cup of tea
served with an ear that pays no heed to the ticking of time.

Spring. Surge of sap through stem and twig;
promise of another cycle –
begetting life from darkest winter,
a glisten of dawns on the hill of Doneen.

God of the Ocean – of life unseen but no less real,
God of the Sun – kindling a glow in hearts that beat for each other,
God of the Earth – of all who till, sow and reap,
God of the Wind – of the air that guards our planet.
God of the Mountain – looking downwards but never down,
offering hope to those who strive for the summit.
God of the Valley – tranquillity ripples in your rivers and streams.

Shinnagh, Cnoc na Locha,
Ranaleen, Caherbreagh –
a leaven of new life on the hill of Doneen.

As the deer reacts to the scent of gorse fire,
our God is alert to our prayer in faith,
for what today brings to us
is related to what we have given
to each of our yesterdays.

Shinnagh, Cnoc na Locha,
new love is always young.
Ranaleen, Caherbreagh –
unique as those in the throes of its joy
bringing new life to the hill of Doneen.

Preface - A Scent of Music

Some childhood events take up residence in the memory forever.

The farewell party for emigrants to the United States up to the late 1950's was referred to as an American Wake because, up until then, many of them would never return. One such memory for me was the all-night hooley for my mother's youngest brother Denny's emigration to California. I was about nine years of age and I'll never forget how I was drawn to the music of The Master, Pádraig O'Keeffe.

Denny was a piper and melodeon player and, along with his late brothers Dan and Mike, would tell me stories of the music masters and other legends of the area, such as the poet Ned 'ten bob' Buckley who regularly won the ten-shillings prize for humorous verse in the Cork Examiner. At the time of the above wake I knew that Pádraig learned from Tom Billy (Murphy) who had learned from Tadhgín an Asal (Tadhgín Ó'Buachalla). Pádraig had been a National teacher but threw it aside to follow his heart's desire in music and the whiskey-and-porter lifestyle that went with it. That night, he played a number of instruments; a tin whistle, a flute, Denny's melodeon and of course his fiddle which he lovingly called 'the wife'.

At that time, and for years until his death, Pádraig taught children from the Paps to Knights Mountain how to play the fiddle. He wasn't fussy about personal hygiene; he showered when caught out in the rain and had a bath if he found himself unexpectedly in a river. By the time I heard the story of the Pied Piper of Hamelin, I was wonderfully aware of the power of good music when played by a happy troubadour.

A Scent Of Music

A tribute to Pádraig O'Caoimh, Master fiddler of Sliabh Luachra.

That's a lot of music out of four little strings,
I remarked when the master played
on the night of my uncle's American wake.

Out in the dairy where a barrel of porter was
tapped was where I had followed,
though he stank like a puck
that had slept in the slops of a pub.

That's a lot of respect out of one little boy;
they stopped calling me "master" after this mastered me,
he said, as he raised up a ponny of porter.

Then he asked if ever I'd felt
the throb of the music dance in my heart and my head
and he took my boy's arm in a hand
big as an antler and pliant
as the tongue of a doe.

So I asked him to fiddle a double St. Patrick,
a jig that I danced as Tom Sweeney had taught
to float on the swell of the music, and never
sit back on my heels in a lazy dance.

He said that a lad who can lather a flagstone,
and still keep time kicking shapes in the air,
has to feel that old spell when a tune in the marrow
gets into the fingers and out through the bow.

He sat me into the smell of his knee,
and fitted the fiddle under my chin,
and we soared, and swooped and hovered
in 'the Coolin',
as he rested
the brush of his face against mine.

Then he changed his tune again
and I found myself within
the wild rhythm of a hornpipe he had made up for the night.
I could feel it as he played, each cadence, every lilt
through his fingers as they tittled up and down the strings.
Then a concertina joined
and another fiddle whined,
as two pupils of the master settled in to play in time.
Very soon we heard encore from the yard outside the door
for a polka on the flagstones underneath the stars.

The devil is in the porter
and Heaven in the music,
he said to the players who had gathered.
So he swallowed the devil
and offered up slow airs
to warrant a passage to Heaven.

A rascal, a genius,
the heart of Sliabh Luachra,
the soul of a Master in music.

Lullaby

Muire
more than mother
fed the world to me
in bits of hard and easy

River
more than water
moonlight gilded whispers
that in daytime danced in ripples

Mozart
more than music
soaring in a thousand ways
through heaven

Fervour
more than eye or ear
can see or hear
more than satisfaction

Desire
more than yearning
for mirages, but a vision
of life brimmed with living

Lover
more than the promise
of hopes I did not know
I dreamed

Tommy Frank O'Connor was born in Currow, Co. Kerry in 1944. He is the author of a novel for adults, *The Poacher's Apprentice* (Marino, 1997); a novel for children, *Kee Kee Cup and Tok* (Wynkin deWorde, 2004); a short story collection, *Loose Head* (DOGHOUSE, 2004) and a poetry collection, *Attic Warpipes* (Bradshaw Books, 2005). His pageant for the stage, *Bréanainn*, was presented by Siamsa Tíre – The National Folk Theatre of Ireland in 1996. Other works for the stage incude a full length play, *Changing Patrick* and several pantomimes.

He is current Clan File of the O'Connor Kerry Clan. O'Connor represented Ireland in the 2005/2006 Away With Words / Words Unbound International Poetry tour. Poetry Ireland / Éigse Eireann's Writers In Schools list includes him as a member as does the Irish Writers' Union and The Society of Irish Playwrights.

Awards for his writings include the Francis MacManus Award (RTE); the Johnathan Swift Award; the Cecil Day Lewis; Crann 2003; Tavistock and Athlone. He was shortlisted for the Sunday Tribune/Hennessy Award in 1998.

Also available from DOGHOUSE:

Heart of Kerry -- an anthology of writing from performers at Poet's Corner, Harty's Bar, Tralee 1992-2003

Song of the Midnight Fox - Eileen Sheehan

Loose Head & Other Stories - Tommy Frank O'Connor

Both Sides Now - Peter Keane

Shadows Bloom / Scáthanna Faoi Bhláth - haiku by John W. Sexton, translations into Irish by Gabriel Rosenstock

FINGERPRINTS (On Canvas) - Karen O'Connor

Vortex - John W. Sexton

Apples In Winter - Liam Aungier

The Waiting Room - Margaret Galvin

I Met A Man... Gabriel Rosenstock

The DOGHOUSE book of Ballad Poems

The Moon's Daughter - Marion Moynihan

Whales Off The Coast Of My Bed - Margaret O'Shea

Every DOGHOUSE book costs €12, postage free, to anywhere in the world
(& other known planets). Cheques, Postal Orders (or any legal method)
payable to DOGHOUSE, also PAYPAL (www.paypal.com) to
doghousepaypal@eircom.net
*"Buy a full set of DOGHOUSE books, in time they will be
collectors' items"* - Gabriel Fitzmaurice, April 12, 2005.
DOGHOUSE
P.O. Box 312
Tralee G.P.O.
Tralee
Co. Kerry
Ireland
tel + 353 6671 37547
email doghouse312@eircom.net   www.doghousebooks.ie